Future Tense

For Robert Swoboda —
warm regards —
Roger Kimball

Future Tense
The Lessons of Culture
in an Age of Upheaval

edited by

Roger Kimball

ENCOUNTER BOOKS
NEW YORK · LONDON

Introduction and Selection © 2012 by Roger Kimball; the individual chapters, the individual authors

First American edition published in 2012 by Encounter Books, an activity of Encounter for Culture and Education, Inc., a nonprofit, tax exempt corporation.

Encounter Books website address: www.encounterbooks.com

Manufactured in the United States and printed on acid-free paper. The paper used in this publication meets the minimum requirements of ANSI/NISO Z39.48?1992 (R 1997) (*Permanence of Paper*).

FIRST AMERICAN EDITION

LIBRARY OF CONGRESS CATALOGING-IN-PUBLICATION DATA

    Future tense : the lessons of culture in an age of upheaval / edited by Roger Kimball.
      p.   cm.
      Includes index.
      ISBN 978-1-59403-634-7 (hardcover : alk. paper)—ISBN 978-1-59403-647-7 (ebook) 1. United States—Civilization—21st century. 2. Civilization, Modern—21st century. I. Kimball, Roger, 1953–
    E169.12.F89 2012
    973.932—dc23   2012017483

Contents

TABLE OF CONTENTS

Introduction

*It was soon discovered that the forms of a free, and the
ends of an arbitrary Government, were things not altogether incompatible.*
—Edmund Burke, *Thoughts on the Cause of the Present
Discontents*

*To fit in with the change of events words, too, had to
change their usual meanings.*
—Thucydides, *History of the Peloponnesian War, Book III*

WRITING IN THE EARLY 1960s, towards the end of
his life, Evelyn Waugh had this to say about Rud-
yard Kipling's reputation as a "conservative":

> [H]e believed civilization to be something laboriously
> achieved which was only precariously defended. He wanted
> to see the defenses fully manned and he hated the liberals
> because he thought them gullible and feeble, believing in
> the easy perfectibility of man and ready to abandon the work
> of centuries for sentimental qualms.

That Burkean appreciation of the fragility of civilization—the insight that our enabling cultural habits and
institutions must constantly be renewed or fail—has always
been at the heart of *The New Criterion's* critical mission.

Civilization, we knew, was not a gift, it was an achievement, difficult of attainment, but all-to-easy to forfeit. The barbarians who would tear it down were not only at the gates but deep within us. As Waugh, writing at the end of the 1930s, put it: "we are all potential recruits for anarchy."

The work of preserving society is sometimes onerous, sometimes almost effortless. The more elaborate the society, the more vulnerable it is to attack, and the more complete its collapse in case of defeat. At a time like the present it is notably precarious. If it falls we shall see not merely the dissolution of a few joint-stock corporations, but of the spiritual and material achievements of our history.

In the Spring of 2011, as we prepared for the thirtieth anniversary of *The New Criterion*, we wanted to put this Burkean theme at the center of our activities. *Future Tense: The Lessons of Culture in an Age of Upheaval* is the result. Every age thinks itself uniquely privileged and uniquely problematic. But as we look back across history, we recognize certain periods in which inherited habits and institutions are suddenly unsettled in a fundamental way—those "plastic moments" that Karl Marx talked about, when many taken-for-granted assumptions about the configuration of social and the shared values that order our lives together seem curiously up for grabs.

It was out sense that we in America, in the West generally, are in the midst of such a revolution in sentiment. Many commentators have dilated on the place that the still reverberating economic crisis of 2008 plays in this drama. The very word "economics" seems to many laymen curiously abstract and distant, a matter merely of dollars and cents. It has turned out—what writers like Hayek already knew—that economics is as much about dolors and sense as it is about money. The main issue, we saw, was the perception of uneasiness, of anxiety. "Future tense," as I put it below in "The Lessons of Culture": "not just subsequent, but also fraught."

The law; the economy; the political prospects; changes in our intellectual habits wrought by changes in our technology; the destiny that is demography: America, the West, indeed the entire world in the early years of the twenty-first century, seems curiously unsettled. Things we had taken for granted seem suddenly up for grabs in some fundamental if still-difficult-to-grasp way. Fissures open among the confidences we had always assumed—in "the market," in national identity, in the basics of social order and cultural value. Future tense: the always hazardous art of cultural prognostication seems brittler now, more uneasy, more tentative.

In this series of eleven essays, earlier versions of which first appeared in *The New Criterion* from September 2011 through June 2012, we have endeavored to provide a kind of critical collage that pictures not only the many challenges America's faces today but also that explores some traditional sources of strength that we may have unfairly neglected or underestimated. The aim of the series, and of this book, is partly to provide a cultural pathologist's report on America and the West's recent trajectory, and also to provide some tonic admonitory counsel about recapturing the civilizational vitality that seems, in many respects, to have ebbed away. Taken together, the essays that compose *Future Tense* seek to reaffirm *The New Criterion*'s commitment to fostering the enabling resources of tradition, the abiding claims of that "common culture" T. S. Eliot fought resolutely to preserve.

Roger Kimball
July 2012

America Resumed:
9/11 Remembered

Michael J. Lewis

IF ASKED TO the cultural legacy of World War I, you might cite Hemingway's *A Farewell to Arms* or George M. Cohan's rousing but now forgotten "Over There." Or perhaps the poignant battle monuments of the American Expeditionary Force, of which Paul Cret's temple at Chateau Thierry is the loveliest. But these items are tangible, and the most vital cultural legacy of any war—or any great national trauma, for that matter—is intangible. It is the comprehensive way it changes our shared attitudes and assumptions, our collective sensibility.

Changes in the collective sensibility, being invisible, usually do not reveal themselves until they are expressed in action. The whip can crack before anyone realizes that it was coiling, and so it was at the end of World War I with Prohibition. In 1919 two separate forces—a wartime mood of urgency and a newfound bitterness toward America's brewers, nearly all of them German—fatefully converged, and in a matter of days accomplished what a half century of temperance crusading had failed to do. Any reckoning of the cultural legacy of the war must give Prohibition a central place.

And what of September 11, 2001? Here too one must distinguish between tangible and intangible consequences. The day has already brought forth an enormous trove of cultural artifacts, including skyscrapers and memorials, novels and films, plays and songs. If they do not quite stand comparison with the achievement of Hemingway, Cohan, or Cret, they are notable for a very different reason. Questions of art and culture seldom are directly involved in a national trauma; they belong to the shadow realm in which great events are digested and replayed after the fact, much as a dream imaginatively rehearses the happenings of the day. But on September 11, it happened that a work of art, a modernist landmark known throughout the world, was at the center of events. And so the cultural artifacts created in the wake of its destruction speak with unusual clarity about how the collective sensibility has changed, and how it has not.

That it would change was taken for granted. Before the sun set on September 11, it was already a commonplace that the attacks would "change everything," as the phrase of the day went. How precisely this would happen was not entirely clear. Roger Rosenblatt, in a widely noted essay in *Time,* suggested that it would bring about the end of irony (an era of neo-sincerity presumably succeeding that of ironic detachment). Surely so violent a shock to the national consciousness must somehow change that consciousness itself.

Or so it was believed, for it was universally sensed that the events of the day represented something new in human experience. Through almost all of human history the scope of collective experience was limited by two strict physical limits, by how far the human voice could reach and by how many people could be squeezed into a given space. Plato's ideal number of 5040 male citizens for a democracy is a realistic figure, given the acoustic properties of a Greek theater and the requirement that citizens take active part in debate—even in our lifetimes few theaters or opera houses have surpassed it.

In the last century, technology made possible a new kind of collective experience that was no longer subject to physical limits. At first blush, one might guess that to experience an event by way of radio or television is to diminish its force. Everyone knows how different it is to watch the same movie at home and in a theater, where your laughter or tension is intensified by the breathing and moving (or perhaps even perspiring) of countless bodies around you. But the new kind of social unity that modern media made possible—a social unity that existed in time but not in space—had distinctive qualities and powers all its own. We are still learning what that means.

This was demonstrated in startling fashion in September 1927, just a few years into the era of radio broadcasting, at the famous Gene Tunney–Jack Dempsey heavyweight championship. In the climactic seventh round, a barrage of punches felled Tunney, to the evident surprise of Dempsey, who stood watching for a moment before retreating to his corner. Until he did, the referee could not begin his count, and the hesitation gave Tunney time to rally and eventually to win the fight. This delay, known to history as the "long count," has been called the most exciting sports moment of the century. It marks the first time the entire nation experienced a simultaneous emotional unity in what we now describe as "real time." So novel was the experience, and so unbearable the suspense, that, according to Frederick Lewis Allen's *Only Yesterday,* five Americans died of heart attacks as they waited for the count.

Experiences of this intensity are usually limited to sports and entertainment events, where the camera and audience are already in place, which is almost never the case with dramatic news events. The Apollo moon landing was a rare exception. Most of the grave national crises of our era—the assassinations of the 1960s or the terrorist attacks of recent years—have been experienced in terms of somber announcements by commentators. But the attacks of September 11 put cameras and audience together at the very vortex of events. Because of the site of the Twin Towers at the southern prow of Manhattan, their death throes could be transmitted live, almost from the first moment, and as they happened—so that one was not buffered by the filter of a detached commentator, who in this instance was every bit as shocked and speechless as the viewer.

Violent acts such as bombings or shootings tend to be swift events, and it is usually only the grisly aftermath that finds its way to television. But the prolonged destruction of the World Trade Center, from the televised airplane impact to the final shuddering collapses, offered prolonged images of unusual graphic clarity. Historical events, even those of the most momentous significance, can rarely be summed up with the visual concision of a billboard or logo, but in their way the death spasms of these buildings were obscenely telegenic.

In one other respect was the experience without precedent: the destruction was witnessed by an audience with an acute and immediate sense of personal danger, a fact that is not sufficiently appreciated. To watch the suffering of others from a safe distance is one thing; it is quite another if you feel you might well be next. Well into that day, newscasts continued to repeat rumors of another hijacked jet still airborne, and so long as they did, one could not be sure that the attacks were finished and that worse was not in store. Until it became clear later that evening that the bolt had been shot and that no more were forthcoming, everyone was in effect imperiled and, at least from a psychological standpoint, stood on the front line.

Those who later tried to describe the pathos of the scene often descended to bathos. The most revolting analysis came in a radio interview with Karlheinz Stockhausen, the German modernist composer, with the *Norddeutscher Rundfunk*. Among his ramblings was this widely quoted gem:

> What happened there is—and now you all have to adjust your minds—the greatest work of art that has ever been. That minds could accomplish in one act, what we in music could never imagine—that people could practice like crazy for ten years, totally fanatically, and then die—this is the greatest work of art that has ever existed in the entire universe.

Although morally contemptible (and quickly withdrawn), Stockhausen's remark had a certain logic. The 9/11 experience inadvertently had many of the properties of a performance—its compression on a television screen, its bold graphic character, and even its symmetrical formal structure—two fireballs and two collapses. Of course, these are pseudo-artistic qualities, and fortuitous ones at that, which have nothing to do with art. But after a half century during which the most progressive artists had sought to abolish any meaningful boundary between art and life, Stockhausen could offer no coherent argument why the attacks were not a sublime performance piece. Ever since Robert Rauschenberg famously erased a de Kooning drawing in 1953, and proposed that the methodical elimination of a work of art might itself constitute an artistic performance, even a heroic negation might be considered as art. Since then, such ambitious negations have increasingly been the substance of fashionable art. The late Philip

Rieff termed such creations *deathworks,* his coinage for works of art that represented "an all-out assault upon something vital to the established culture."

If it is outrageous to speak of the September 11 attacks as art, their indelible graphic images could not help but affect the art that followed, or—to put it more precisely— to interfere with the creation of that art. Great art has the capacity to distill complex and abstract themes into an image of graphic clarity, so that the imagination might grasp them, in the way that Michelangelo's turbulent *Last Judgment* focuses the mind on the final issues of death, judgment, and eternity. But the destruction of the World Trade Center took place in a moment of absolute graphic clarity beyond which no further distillation was possible. In itself it was a *Last Judgment.* And so the graphic after-image of the attacks, indelible to anyone who saw it, pre-cludes the open-ended search for form that is the task of visual art.

It did not take long for this to become apparent. Late in 2002, Rockefeller Center installed Eric Fischl's bronze sculpture *Tumbling Woman,* which depicted a robust nude woman falling headfirst, just touching the ground with the top of her head—in other words, at the instant of impact. The obvious subject was the two hundred or so victims who, their backs to the inferno, leapt to their deaths from the upper stories of the World Trade Center. By obsessively revisiting these plunging figures, Fischl seems to have been seeking to expunge his private grief, but without asking if this private exercise was a fit subject for public art. The public reaction was much the same that met Stockhausen—disbelieving revulsion—and the work was speedily whisked out of sight.

Even if an artist could scrupulously efface every last vestige of the televised images, their implicit psychological associations remained, and, try as he might, whatever else the artist might wish to express would be overpowered by these associations. This was the conclusion of the German artist Thomas Eller, who perceptively summed up the problem: "Many artists shy away from 9/11 because with 9/11 it is immediately clear that the emotional power does not come from the artist."

If artists could steer clear of 9/11, architects did not have that luxury. The architects who squared off in the fall 2002 competition to design the new World Trade Center had to tackle head on the iconic status of the original towers, and try to match their visual power. Of course, the task was impossible. Nothing could be more understated than the terse Minimalism of the original towers, as laconic as a pyramid, and nothing could pack more graphic punch than those towers in their final agonies. Making matters worse is the natural desire of architects to make their designs stand out from the crowd, especially in large open competitions where one must catch the eye of the jurors with bold forms that carry well at a distance.

The result was that the 400-odd submissions fidgeted with the fervor and the desperate eagerness to please that one usually associates with kindergarteners. Some fidgeted tastefully, such as Norman Foster who proposed a pair of rounded towers that gently touched one another in the air, as if for reassurance. And others fidgeted bombastically, such as the team headed by Richard Meier, the architect of the Getty Museum, which envisioned a gridded superblock with open squares cut through it, a kind of vertical tic-tac-toe board.

To be fair, the architects had been dealt a bad hand. Strong buildings come from strong clients, which the builders of the new World Trade Center most emphatically were not. Responsibility for the project was divided between the owner of the property (the Port Authority of New York City), the lessee (Larry Silverstein), and the Lower Manhattan Development Corporation, which the state and city had jointly created to oversee the development of the site. Only a single client building for himself can make the concise list of practical needs that is the essence of a good architectural program. Sprawling committees cannot, certainly not that shotgun marriage of politicians, developers, and bureaucrats. And so the architectural program listed only generalities, of which the mandate to "restore the skyline" and to preserve the footprints of the towers were the decisive factors. This made the competition a performance in skyline acrobatics, rather than an exercise in the thoughtful making of space, what Louis Kahn once described as the essence of architecture.

When Daniel Libeskind finally won the competition in early 2003, it was as much for his resumé as for his actual submission. His Jewish Museum in Berlin, with its splintered geometry and tortuous paths of movement, had been an international sensation and had given him the reputation of a master of intellectual pathos. For the World Trade Center, he returned again to the motif of splintered geometry, although now he inverted its meaning. At Berlin, the thwarted paths and broken forms spoke of tragic incomprehensibility; in Manhattan they were to be gestures of triumph, culminating in a spiraling 1,776-foot-high Freedom Tower that ostentatiously invoked the Statue of Liberty. At its base was to be a monumental Wedge of Light that was to be aligned astronomically, like Stonehenge, so that every September 11, for the precise 102 minutes of the attack, "the sun will shine without shadow, in perpetual tribute to altruism and courage." This combination of graphic and rhetorical pizzazz was winning, and, once endorsed by Ada Louise Huxtable and a pageant of other critics and historians, it won handily.

Judged simply on visual criteria, as a display of architectural rendering, Libeskind's proposal was stunning, although one needed to imagine viewing it from the bottom of that canyon of glass. One suspects it would be rather like Coleridge's description of the Russian palace of ice, "glittering, cold, and transitory." At the heart of Libeskind's project was a certain philosophical incoherence, not to say insincerity. The patriotic patter that accompanied his Freedom Tower design had no intrinsic relationship to his trademark Deconstructivist geometry, which until recently had little to do with altruism, courage, or any traditional moral qualities whatsoever. In fact, Libeskind's quarrel seemed to be with tradition itself. His animus extended even to the right angle, which he proclaimed in 1999 had "originated in Egypt from the division of land—mine versus yours," and therefore had no place in contemporary life. Such puckish intellectual games are fine for the classroom but not for a commemorative site of national tragedy. In short order, the public realized that Libeskind was not quite the bargain he had been sold as and set about repairing the damage.

A strong client emerged at last when Silverstein took control of the project that, after all, he was paying for. He wrested the commission from Libeskind and put it in the hands of David Childs, a seasoned architect with experience in skyscrapers. Libeskind was relegated to the largely symbolic role of master planner. Childs briskly went about untangling the geometry of the tower, and giving it a needed bit of Egyptian rectilinearity. In its radically simplified and clarified form, it now rises from a square base, modulates through elegant chamfers into an octagon, and returns to a square at the summit. The result has something of the cool, self-effacing simplicity of the original towers without being an imitation. As it nears completion this fall, it seems far less likely to date than Libeskind's deconstructivist geometries, which already read as somewhat musty relics of the 1990s. In the end, even the name Freedom Tower was quietly shelved, perhaps in recognition that the building is not quite the all-glass celebration of freedom and openness that Libes-kind had promised. It now wears a bombproof carapace around its lower ten stories, like a suit of body armor, reminding us that what was once a target remains a target.

Stockhausen, Fischl, and Libeskind, each in his own way, had come up against a transformed public sensibility that they no longer recognized. Accustomed as they were to adulation and critical respect for their transgressive gestures, they were caught off guard by the intensity of the public wrath. Heretofore there had been no indication that transgressive gestures were anything but a smart career move. After all, those artists who had run afoul of the public in recent decades and been threatened with censorship, from Robert Mapplethorpe to Chris Ofili, had been handsomely rewarded with approving editorials and skyrocketing prices. There is a useful German term for those who make a career out of scandalizing the bourgeoisie—*Bürgerschreck*—although the American version was less likely to be an anarchist provocateur than a canny hustler. But in the wake of 9/11, the public's willingness to humor *Bürgerschreck* antics, at least when they touched on the tragedy, had been drastically reduced.

The one thing the public did demand, and in the most vehement terms, was a solemn and respectful memorial to the dead. Here, for once, the authorities moved efficiently, selecting a design in 2003 and rushing it through to completion this month, although at the rather astonishing cost of nearly half a billion dollars. It now opens as the National September 11 Memorial & Museum at the World Trade Center, and, in many respects, it is commendable. It has a austere dignity appropriate to its site and character: within the footprints of the towers, a perpetual internal waterfall flows, surrounded by stone tablets on which are incised the names of the dead. The flowing water gives a welcome living note to what would otherwise be a place of nearly unbearable oppressiveness.

With its air of tragic dignity, the September 11 Memorial is better than might have been expected. It is certainly superior to such recent memorials as those to Franklin Delano Roosevelt or the Korean War, each of which arrays its sculptural figures to form pious visual anecdotes. (It is also superior to the more conventional memorials built at the Pentagon and at Shanksville, where United Airlines Flight 93 crashed.) But it suffers from a confusion of means and ends. It speaks almost exclusively of the physical loss of the buildings that stood there, and inadequately about those who suffered and died there, and who are represented only by their incised names. Michael Arad, the designer of the memorial, had no choice in the matter. He merely followed the terms of the competition program, which mandated the preservation of the building footprints, which meant that the central lesson would be the fact of their violent destruction.

In this one discerns the hand of Maya Lin, the designer of America's most successful modern memorial, the Vietnam Veterans Memorial in Washington, and the most prominent member of the building committee for the September 11 Memorial. It is no coincidence that her own memorial and Arad's are both essays in absence, in which a mournful emptiness is placed at the center and offset by somber passages of black wall. But in Washington, the void is symbolic and abstractly expressive, while in New York it is painfully literal, the memorialization of an actual ruin, something rather different from the physical embodiment of an abstract idea. In the end, there is something distressing about making a monument out of a calamitous national defeat. After all, what country builds monuments to its defeats? The central monuments of the world's great cities—the Nelson Column, the Vendôme Column, the *Siegessäule*—are monuments to victories; the defeats are acknowledged and mourned quietly elsewhere.

Admittedly, the September 11 Memorial helps give focus and voice to the nation's sorrow. But sorrow is only one tone in the spacious emotional register of a nation, and there are others, such as resolution, defiance, and even fury, that at certain times might be more appropriate. A person who could grieve but not snarl or even bite would be a strangely limited creature, and the same is true of a nation. Yet, after September 11, the public was given copious outlets only for its sorrow and none at all for its fury. (One must make the necessary exception for country and western music.)

When it came to addressing the harder and more fiery sentiments of the public, the cultural apparatus acted as bridle rather than spur, and rather nervously at that. Anything that might serve to focus national rage, such as showing films of the burning towers and plunging victims, was swept from the airwaves after a few days, only to be shown in short, carefully edited passages during the occasional anniversary broadcast or documentary. This was rationalized as a measure to spare bereft family members further grief, but it is much more the sense that such imagery was deemed incendiary, and likely to stoke the flames of public wrath, as if the most urgent danger—and the only danger—facing America was the prospect of mass mob violence against American Muslims.

Most shameful in this respect was Hollywood, which is perhaps the organ of American culture that has changed least in outlook and sensibility since September 11. Not only did it not change but, with a few notable exceptions, it did not seem to recognize that the rest of the country had. Otherwise, how can producers have believed that there would be a mass market for films in which American soldiers were sent to meaningless slaughter (*Lions for Lambs,* 2007), or killed one of their own (*In the Valley of Elah,* 2007), or raped a teenager (*Redacted,* 2009)? Needless to say, all were embarrassing flops, as was *Rendition* (2007), which was also sharply critical of the American war effort. By the time *The Hurt Locker* (2010) appeared, a war film in which the soldier protagonists were actually shown sympathetically and in all their human complexity, the public stayed away, no longer believing Hollywood capable of making a film in which American soldiers were not the bad guys.

Nor was the film industry capable of making pictures in which Muslim terrorists *were* the bad guys. Film is a medium that is peculiarly suited for the depiction of villainy, yet Muslim villains are strikingly absent from Hollywood films (except when working as our agents). Oliver Stone's *World Trade Center* (2006) accomplished the peculiar feat of being the only major film about the destruction of the twin towers—without showing that destruction. It depicted the claustrophobic ordeal of two transit policemen caught in the wreckage of the towers, an act of literary editing that managed to turn a story of terrorism and murder into a generic survival story. Had Stone been willing to speculate freely about conspiracies, as in his *JFK*, one could imagine him making a very different kind of film, say about the shadowy Iranian role in the attacks. Obviously, such a project would be unthinkable.

Even a film that was explicitly about terrorism, *A Mighty Heart* (2007)—Michael Winterbottom's treatment of the kidnapping and beheading of Daniel Pearl—followed Stone's example in refusing to show violent terrorists. In fact, the only explicit act of violence in the film is the torture of a suspected terrorist at the behest of his Pakistani and American captors. One could not even defend this on the grounds that it is evenhanded—of the "pox on both your houses" variety—for the film's American subjects are corrupt or evil while the only terrorists shown are treated as pathetic flunkies.

The truth is that because Hollywood is America's most important contribution to international culture it is simultaneously the least national—in terms of point of view—of any American cultural organ and least able to express distinctly national attitudes. This development has long been in the making, ever since American films began to earn most of their receipts from overseas viewing. Typically a modern Hollywood blockbuster earns two-thirds or more of its profits overseas, and any film with explicitly nationalist content is seen to threaten those profits. If September 11 created a demand for cathartic films in which Americans squared off against foreign enemies, Hollywood was not about to meet it. In fact, the industry's dread of offending the international market seems only to have intensified, to judge from the fate of the remake of *Red Dawn*. The original 1984 film was an escapist fantasy in which American high school students conduct guerrilla warfare against Soviet and Cuban invaders. The new version updated the villains to Communist Chinese, but in post-production the squeamish

MGM studio insisted on digitally altering the enemy to be the one country in the world in which American films are not screened: North Korea.

Hollywood once was not always thus. On December 7, 1941, the musical comedy *Holiday Inn* was halfway through shooting, but its Independence Day number, where Fred Astaire's famously dances to exploding fire-crackers, was completely reedited to include filmed footage of President Roosevelt, General MacArthur, and the United States military. It was in theaters before the summer was out. By contrast it was five years before the appearance of Paul Greengrass's *United 93*, a heartbreaking and forensic recreation of the passenger uprising that led to the plane's crash. Even then, audiences seeing previews were recorded as having shouted in dismay, "too soon, too soon!" Too late, they might better have said.

Actually, when it wants to, Hollywood is still able to turn on a dime. Less than three months after the killing of Osama bin Laden on May 2, Kathryn Bigelow, the director of *The Hurt Locker*, announced that the SEAL team's extraordinary mission would be the subject of her next film—that The White House was offering unprecedented access. As well it might: the film is scheduled to open one month before the presidential election next year and will highlight the one accomplishment of the Obama presidency over which no one, at least no American, quibbles.

It is well and good that Hollywood would celebrate an American feat of arms without qualification or apology. But why has it taken ten years? The killing of Osama was hardly the first such feat. Since 2003, nine Congressional Medals of Honor have been awarded for just the kind of bravery that Hollywood once celebrated in Sergeant York or Audie Murphy. The circuitous way in which Hollywood and other sectors of American culture have addressed the attacks of September 11—lingering on some aspects, touching gingerly on others, and steering widely clear of yet others—suggests the presence of a taboo, like one of those massive but invisible astronomical objects that announce its presence only indirectly, by deflecting the light that passes through it or by affecting the movement of other objects. When it comes to September 11, the taboo seems to lie in the unambiguously national context of the event.

The buildings and institutions that were targeted on that day were chosen as symbols of American national identity; those who were murdered were not collateral casualties but were killed in their capacity as Americans. The entire framework of the attack was a deliberate and focused assault on those objects that stood for the American government and American capitalism. (Although the target of United 93 is sometimes said to have been the White House, it was surely headed for the United States Capitol, a far more conspicuous—and realistic—target for a novice pilot). But if the context of the event was explicitly American, this was precisely the terrain on which the arbiters of American culture—at least a substantial faction—felt themselves uneasy. Feelings of national solidarity, the sense of personal participation in the fate of one's nation-state, have so long been disparaged as jingoism that even those artists who felt unaccountable patriotic stirrings found themselves utterly unable to make artistic use of them.

When one comes eyeball to eyeball with a shocking and malignant truth, but is unable to speak frankly and openly about it because of a taboo, one must resort to distortion, evasion, and self-deception. Surely the saddest example of this—and there are many—is the peculiar September 11 comic book by Art Spiegelman, called *In the Shadow of No Towers* (2004). Known for his frequent *New*

Yorker covers, Spiegelman first won fame for his graphic novel *Maus,* which told the story of Nazi death camps in terms of cats and mice. On September 11, he was only a few blocks from Ground Zero and witnessed the destruction at first hand, in what was clearly a day of overpowering horror, of fear, rage, and confusion. But when it came to giving visual form to these feelings, he flinched. He showed a tableau of violent scenes, including the toppling of the Statue of Liberty, the slitting of the throat of the American eagle, and the dowsing of children with burning oil—and showed those acts being performed by President Bush, Vice President Cheney, and Uncle Sam.

In his litany of crimes, Spiegelman was quite accurate. Each of these specific gruesome acts did take place on September 11: a tall structure was toppled, the throats of pilots were cut, and a great many of the innocent were immolated in burning fuel oil. But in Spiegelman's rendition, these acts were assigned to American perpetrators and not to Muslim terrorists, recasting the story with permissible villains so that the taboo might remain intact. In an age of upheaval and crisis, when cherished certainties must be discarded and suppressed truths voiced, one is grateful for the artist who can do so imaginatively and fearlessly. But in this respect Spiegelman, like many of his counterparts, was the opposite of King Lear's Fool—instead of removing masks and puncturing taboos, his comic book about September 11 worked nervously and diligently to see that they were firmly in place.

Yet another lesson of culture after September 11 is that one must not fret or mope. This is hardly the first time that a sizable branch of the cultural establishment has failed to draw the appropriate lessons from new events. Yesterday's radicals become today's purveyors of the conventional wisdom and tomorrow's sclerotic academicians.

But even immovable objects can be useful. It was the resistance of an academic establishment that gave the necessary hard surface against which early modernism needed to recoil. This is why T. S. Eliot, in his "Notes Towards the Definition of Culture" insisted strongly on "the vital importance for a society of *friction* between its parts." If friction was damaging to a machine, it was essential to the metabolism of a living society:

> both class and region, by dividing the inhabitants of a country into two different kinds of groups, lead to a conflict favourable to creativeness and progress. And ... these are only two of an indefinite number of conflicts and jealousies which should be profitable to society. Indeed, the more the better: so that everyone should be an ally of everyone else in some respects, and an opponent in several others, and no one conflict, envy or fear will dominate.

Eliot was opposed to totalitarianism, cultural or otherwise, and one suspects he would have seen the contentious readjustment of values, aspirations, and delusions after September 11 as a sign of health—the necessary and positive signs of a living body in the process of healthful and boisterous change.

Change, of course, does not progress at a uniform or constant rate. My old college drama teacher liked to say that amateur playwrights tend to make their characters change too easily. Real change occurs seldom, and there are only four motivations for plausibly changing a character: love, prolonged pain or suffering, getting what you want, and finding out that nothing is as you had believed. On September 11, America found that much of what it believed was not true: the end of the Cold War did not bring about what was once touchingly described as "The End of History"; the process of globalization, in which so much hope was invested, did not necessarily lead to increased good will or security; and the fact that we as a nation wished no nation ill by no means ensured that no nation wished us ill.

Those revelations, administered in the most brutal manner conceivable, have reshaped the collective consciousness of the nation. But they have done so with very little help from art, which through the ages has been the most effective instrument for focusing the cultural consciousness, for framing its questions and concerns in the lucid terms without which no national conversation is possible. If art has largely failed to do this, it is partly because the specific nature of the event—the destruction of a physical icon in a way that created an entirely different kind of visual icon—had an impoverishing effect on the formal imagination of artists.

But it is also because of a taboo, imposed gradually and imperceptibly over the past few decades, about expressing strong emotions in national terms—other than that of grief. This offers more concern, for a culture that cannot express, and make sense out of, the longings and passions of the people that sustains that culture cannot remain vital. Solzhenitsyn once said that exile is cruelest to the writer, who, unlike the painter or composer, must be in constant contact with the spoken sound of his own language. If September 11 has shown anything, it is that a similar sort of internal exile has occurred in some portion of the American cultural world. But vanguards that become successful have a tendency to stand still, by which means they sooner or later become the rear-guard.

The cultural legacy of September 11 is a sprawling landscape, but out of the tumult a few salient facts are visible. Its principal objects at Ground Zero, a skyscraper and a national memorial, are quite respectable, and even commendable, given the enormous burden of expectations placed on them. In creative art, there has been distinctly less interest in strategies to *épater les bourgeoisie*. If Hollywood behaved appallingly, it did so at its own expense—not merely financially but also in terms of public prestige. The decade was not remarkable for conspicuous artistic innovation but rather for quiet work. In other words, a plucky nation, after a period of shock and mourning, resumed its fateful course.

Is America Periclean?

Victor Davis Hanson

W HAT MIGHT A contemporary American audience make of their president on Memorial Day complimenting the people on their cultivation of "refinement without extravagance and knowledge without effeminacy"—with an added up-from-the-bootstraps flourish that "wealth, we employ more for use than for show, and place the real disgrace of poverty not in owning to the fact but in declining the struggle against it"?

And would they be further aghast if our Commander-in-Chief turned to foreign affairs in the same self-assured vein: "We have forced every sea and land to be the highway of our daring, and everywhere, whether for evil or for good, have left imperishable monuments behind us"? Would such a president be judged unhinged—either homophobic in applying stereotyped constructs of masculinity, or cold and uncaring in demanding responsibility from the impoverished? Or perhaps triumphalist in assessing military achievement abroad on a material scale rather than an ethical one?

Or would a modern Pericles be hailed for his honesty in touching upon universal human truths that erudition without physicality can soften us, that we are responsible for our own wealth or poverty, and that America should be proud on its confident role abroad?

In truth, it would be hard to imagine an oration more disturbing to the modern American elite's sensibilities than Pericles' majestic funeral oration delivered in the winter of 431/30 B.C. at the end of the first campaigning season of the Peloponnesian War—a masterful summary some 2,500 years old of what once made imperial democratic Athens great and why, in its darkest hours, it would prevail. The unabashed confidence of Pericles in his own civilization and national ethos, and the eloquence by which he conveyed it, were once gold standards for unapologetic Western democratic rhetoricians. Abraham Lincoln and Winston Churchill both emulated the speech's reverence for ancestry, tradition, and cultural exceptionalism as a way of explaining why a confident America or Britain, *in extremis,* deserved its influence and should express it openly beyond its borders.

In our postmodern times, the speech bothers scholars and students, not just for the unabashed values it embraces, but also for the brash tone in which it claims them as uniquely Athenian. The oration might have resonated with the so-called Greatest Generation coming home from victory in Asia and Europe in 1945, but not for subsequent ones, demoralized by Vietnam and awash in material affluence who became convinced that their country was hardly perfect and therefore often not good. More commonly, American elites—as we saw in President Barack Obama's June 4, 2009 speech in Cairo—falsely attribute the undeniable achievements of their civilization to others, and, in schizophrenic fashion, are confused whether to be ashamed of its singular contributions that have led to great wealth and power or to appear magnanimous in fraudulently accrediting its singularity to lesser others.

The Funeral Oration, of course, cannot be altogether appreciated in isolation. The majestic speech was delivered following an initial invasion of Spartan infantry, who, if they had not severely damaged the sacred soil of Attica, had at least humiliated the Athenian rural folk. Many had abandoned their farms to flee inside the city proper. Once inside the walls, the demoralized audience of evacuees—crowded amid unsanitary urban conditions—suffered, the next year, from a horrific epidemic that could be neither explained nor treated. The infamous plague would kill off nearly a quarter of the Athenian population, including Pericles himself. And much more disaster, likewise unforeseen, was on the horizon—the impending infantry defeat at the battle of Delium, the horrific losses in the Sicilian Expedition, and the final victory of Sparta, occasioned by the Spartan admiral Lysander sailing triumphantly into the Piraeus.

It was in the bleak context of the first invasion's aftermath that Pericles accepted the annual obligation of offering words of condolences for the year's war dead. But apparently, contrary to normal custom, he used the dark occasion to transcend epitaphic protocols. Instead, in broader terms, he reminded the demoralized populace not to weaken or give up their glorious city to the Spartans. They had given their obligations to past generations of Athenians who created and then bequeathed their exceptional culture.

The oration is found in the second book of Thucydides' masterful history of the Peloponnesian War, but it still troubles readers for a variety of reasons. Is the stirring speech all Pericles' own, or is the text enhanced somewhat by Thucydides himself—a mix between what the contemporary General Thucydides himself actually heard and transcribed verbatim, and what, as a historian and editor, he felt in retrospect that his hero Pericles should have additionally added on the occasion? No one knows quite for sure, though the soaring phraseology, complex syntax, frequently poetic expression, and often rarified Greek vocabulary suggested that the Funeral Oration would have been as difficult for the average Athenian listener to follow as a reading of a Federalist Paper would be for a contemporary American.

In addition, Thucydides often uses a dark irony in the composition of history. Thus the majestic Funeral Oration is immediately to be followed by horrific accounts of the plague, as if to remind us of how low the once mighty have fallen. By the same token, the Athenian brutality shown to the poor Melians at the end of book five of the history is followed by a long account of catastrophic payback to imperial Athens in Sicily. The Funeral Oration, then, is as much a literary creation as it was Pericles' finest rhetorical moment.

What can this tutorial about national greatness offered by Pericles/Thucydides teach us about the American experience in our present age of uncertainty? The United States is not suffering from either invasion or a lethal plague. The first decade of the new millennium has, nonetheless, proven a time of American despair—the attack of September 11, three ongoing wars in the Middle East, a 2008 financial earthquake, high unemployment, massive annual deficits, unsustainable yet still growing national debt exceeding $14 trillion, widespread disillusionment about the future of American entitlements and energy supplies, worry over a rising China and radical Islam, and doubt about the continuance of civil society itself.

After bemoaning the truth that the public commemoration of brave men should not rest capriciously on the rhetorical skill of a funeral speaker—a trope followed by Lincoln in his Gettysburg address—Pericles begins his speech with Athens's ancestors, thanking them for two contributions. Earlier generations of Athenians had kept Athens safe from foreign and Hellenic aggression, and their sacrifice had allowed a more recent cohort to expand the city-state into an Aegean-wide empire whose benefits Pericles' own generation could enjoy without the toil and danger spent in acquiring it.

The mark of a great leader and an even greater people is precisely such reverence for the past—not a vague past, but one of real people who lived, suffered, achieved, and died for others. In our age of presentism and pride in our high-tech affluence—in which Americans use the standards of the contemporary university to judge prior generations as inferior to our own sensibilities in terms of race, class, and gender equality—such blanket praise of our ancestors seems reactionary and illiberal. After all, the President of the United States has recently apologized for American behavior of a half-century earlier in Iran; for supposed past indifference to the Palestinian issue; for maltreatment of Native Americans, blacks, and other minorities; and for dropping the atomic bomb in World War II. Nowhere does Barack Obama hint that he himself—so unlike the anonymous of the past whom he easily castigates—might lack the physical stamina or bravery to withstand a bout with pre-antibiotic diphtheria, to drive a mule team in summer across the Utah desert, to survive a Banzai charge on Okinawa, or to retreat from the Yalu River in November 1950.

Instead, all the tragedies and physical torment of past generations of Americans are reduced into vague nothingness, and our predecessors have become almost cardboard cutout figures, judged as sympathetic or repellent based on the twenty-first-century politically correct morality of an affluent metrosexual culture which would likely fail the challenges of danger, torment, and hardship that eighteenth- and nineteenth-century Americans routinely overcame. Nowhere do we even attribute the magic of cell phones, jet travel, or modern medicine to an inherited intellectual and scientific foundation that was the legacy of the collective lives of long-dead Americans, who suffered greatly and gave us much.

Pericles' point was not that the Athenians of a distant age who founded the empire were perfect, only that they had bequeathed a powerful Athens that the present generation apparently benefitted from and enjoyed. To fault the gift would be as illogical as it would be ungracious. A modern American update would be to lavish praise on the generations that defeated the British, Mexicans, Spanish, Germans, Italians, Japanese, and Soviets, and thereby passed on a free America, which we find far preferable to the defeats envisioned by our former enemies. The degree to which many Americans were at one time racist, sexist, or brutal would, then, be overshadowed by the fact that they were both better than the alternative of the times and had enough confidence that their own survival—and only their survival—would create the conditions for subsequent self-introspection, critique, and certain moral improvement.

There is also an element of old-fashioned manners in Pericles' speech wholly lacking in modern platitudes: the recipient does not critique the benefactor's gift as being not quite what he might have wished—unless he wishes to refuse it altogether. Or in blunter parlance, a Periclean American president would not have apologized for our fathers' sins because he would have understood that they were dwarfed by the freedom and prosperity that our generation inherited from them.

Indeed, if our American inheritance were so bad, then we would be under no obligation to be tainted by it and could simply refuse the heritage altogether—and at our own, rather than our ancestors', expense. Why not now expand present-day Indian reservations to include entire states where Native Americans could return to their own migratory past and indigenous alternative lifestyles? Why not refuse to use the water, power, or flood prevention capability of a Hoover Dam that so disfigures the natural course of the Colorado River? If modern man had so mindlessly destroyed John Muir's scenic Hetch Hetchy Sierra Nevada valley, why then would not liberal San Franciscans rally to dismantle the dam, or at least today refuse to accept drinking water delivered from such a vast public project of scarifying dams and canals? Pericles' point, of course, is not that a present generation cannot critique prior ones, but that it should do so in a manner that weighs concrete benefits versus abstract burdens.

Pericles next reminds Athenians that

> There are few parts of our dominions that have not been augmented by those of us here, who are still more or less in the vigor of life; while the mother country has been furnished by us with everything that can enable her to depend on her own resources whether for war or for peace.

Unlike Pericles' confident, idealized portrait of an ascendant ancient Athens, the American intelligentsia is mostly apologetic about the formation and growth of the United States, either seeing it as theft of some sort from Native Americans, Spaniards, or Mexicans, or discounting altogether the notion that impressive geography and size are anything in which a sophisticated people can take pride—as if 300 million Americans today do not benefit from a transcontinental nation with coastlines on two oceans and hundreds of millions of acres in between, replete with natural resources. After all, the reason why a suburbanite can work out at an upscale gym or why an inner-city youth sports expensive sneakers has something to do with the vast wheat acreage of the Midwest, the oil and gas of Texas, and the bustling ports of Oakland and Los Angeles that are the dividends of a vast transcontinental America.

Is that diffidence about the source of our generation's present-day coast-to-coast fortune simply a symptom of an affluent and leisured society that can now afford to second-guess its inheritance with the assurance that the bequest is nonetheless secure and not subject to renegotiation? After all, would those who live in San Diego wish it to be governed in a manner as are those in Tijuana? Would today's residents of Arizona prefer that their environs were part of the Mexican province of nearby Sonora? Didn't it prove to be a good thing that millions of people in the American Southwest came to live under the auspices of the United States instead of Mexico? The abstract answer in our university might be no—even as over 11 million Mexican nationals have voted yes with their feet, and another 70 million Americans of the region have seconded that vote by staying put and not fleeing in mirror-image fashion southward to Mexico.

Pericles next touches upon "military achievements which gave us our several possessions," as if the augmentation of Athenian territory was also a good thing rather than a shameful dividend of a bad imperialism. Here, the obvious disconnect with ancient Athens is more rhetorical than real: on campus we might deplore in theory the annexation of a Hawaii or collectively lament the acquisition of a Puerto Rico or Virgin Islands, but there is no contemporary majority willing to give that territory up, either the residents themselves or Americans at large.

In other words, Hawaiians apparently deem themselves better off as Americans, and Americans are happy that our ancestors annexed Hawaii, whether judged in terms of present-day commerce, tourism, or national security. So far, Puerto Rican nationalists have not been able to convince the majority of their fellow islanders to secede from the United States, even though the American government has extended them an opportunity through a willingness to abide by plebiscites on numerous occasions.

Pericles next turns to praise the democratic system of government. Here, his admiration of Athenian equality under the law, the application of equal justice regardless of social standing, and the emphasis on merit rather than wealth or birth is welcome stuff for the modern American egalitarian—even if the Athenian claims an unapologetic exceptionalism on the grounds that "our constitution does not copy the laws of neighboring states; we are rather a pattern to others than imitators ourselves."

Whereas Americans now assume that equality can be perpetually expanded without dire consequences, Pericles anticipates a problem, one innate to free humans in prosperous consensual societies: the spread of license. Almost immediately, he qualifies his praise of radical democracy with this caveat:

> But all this ease in our private relations does not make us lawless as citizens. Against this fear is our chief safeguard, teaching us to obey the magistrates and the laws, particularly such as regard the protection of the injured, whether they are actually on the statute book, or belong to that code which, although unwritten, yet cannot be broken without acknowledged disgrace.

In other words, there can be no endlessly expansionary notion of personal freedom and choice unless laws are sacrosanct and the people remain in fear of transgressing them and incurring public shame. Whether or not Thucydides much later reworked the address in light of the Athenian execution of the Melians and Mytilenes, and the flagrant disregard shown Athenian custom and tradition once the plague finally ripped off the thin veneer of civilization, or had his own subsequent unfair exile at the hands of the rabble-rousing demagogue Cleon in mind is unknown. More certain is that there was no ancient concept of a constantly evolving legal code that bestowed ever more rights and ever fewer responsibilities on the citizen.

"Fear," "unwritten" habits, and shame are powerful checks on unfettered appetites, impediments that Pericles realizes are critical to the maintenance of law in free-wheeling democracies. In today's modern liberal states, there is little commensurate anxiety that for every act there must be a reaction, a zero-sum notion that with greater freedom must come greater self-restraint. Where we fall short here is the peculiarly modern sense that we have become better as a people in striking down discrimination and freeing our laws from race, class, and gender biases. We forget that we are now often worse as individuals—as indicated by rampant crime, the disintegration of the family, or rising illegitimacy rates—than our parents and grandparents, who accepted that Americans should not indulge in what was legally free, but otherwise morally and ethically unwise for a society at large.

Americans are also schizophrenic about their own private wealth or, at least, the public manifestation of their hard-won leisure and affluence. Seeking material rewards as much in the concrete as in the abstract, they find ways of expressing unease with their own good fortune. Yet Pericles unashamedly reminds the Athenians of their own lavishly outfitted city and the material benefits that Athenians enjoy in their private life:

> Further, we provide plenty of means for the mind to refresh itself from business. We celebrate games and sacrifices all the year round, and the elegance of our private establishments forms a daily source of pleasure and helps to banish the spleen; while the magnitude of our city draws the produce of the world into our harbor, so that to the Athenian the fruits of other countries are as familiar a luxury as those of his own.

One of the most unfortunate aspects of contemporary American life is precisely this inability to calibrate the importance of private wealth and the value of material improvement. Instead, our politicians continually harp on the prevalence of Dickensian poverty or the inability of government to ensure absolute parity among the citizenry—without even a Periclean nod to the wonder of American bounty in the age of globalization.

Imagine if George W. Bush or Barack Obama had reminded the nation that we have put into the hands of 300 million Americans the ability to call anyone in the planet in a nanosecond, to Skype a relative without much cost across the continent, or to fly cheaply from state to state in a few hours—all in a mere thirty years, extending opportunities to the entire citizenry, through brilliant new technologies, that were only recently restricted to the very wealthy. Today's welfare recipient's iPhone is superior in performance to the suitcase-sized cell phone that the Wall Street stockbroker of the 1980s used to lug around. Yet have any politicians reminded any American of that fact, of the "magnitude of our city"?

Instead of simply reciting another dreary statistic from another faceless bureaucracy, would that an American leader, in Periclean fashion, remind Americans of the variety of affordable fresh fruit available year round in local supermarkets just blocks from their home, the vast differences in comfort, safety, and ease of use in today's Chevrolet Malibu versus yesterday's coupe, or how the idealized 800-square-foot house of the postwar middle class homeowner is now about the size of a contemporary tract house living room. For Pericles, the beauty of Athens was insidious and permeated all aspects of private life. In contrast, our politicians see us as blessed or cursed to the degree to which government officially or unofficially has lent us aid—even though the great breakthroughs that have so vastly ameliorated American life were always products of the uniquely American free enterprise system and the popular culture that accompanied it, and yet again go uncalibrated in any assessment of relative poverty or affluence.

If we turn to our military policy, there also we differ from our antagonists." So Pericles, in a fashion readily apparent to contemporary Americans—and at that time in obvious contrast with Sparta—brags that Athenians

> throw open our city to the world, and never by alien acts exclude foreigners from any opportunity of learning or observing, although the eyes of an enemy may occasionally profit by our liberality; trusting less in system and policy than to the native spirit of our citizens; while in education, where our rivals from their very cradles by a painful discipline seek after manliness, at Athens we live exactly as we please, and yet are just as ready to encounter every legitimate danger.

This is the classic pragmatic defense of an open and liberal society—its underappreciated profits far outweighing its freely acknowledged debits. Liberality ensures a free-thinking, opportunistic, and self-reliant Athenian that can more than overcome the disadvantages of not safekeeping state secrets or embracing a militarism that would entail a rigid and regimented code of unattractive collective conduct.

If our civil libertarians were to applaud Pericles here, they might recoil in horror that his praise is a preamble for a more ambitious assertion immediately following—namely that the willingness to meet danger by volition rather than coercion creates a more effective military that is more often victorious in war. Whereas we might praise individual choice and freedom as enhancements of civic society, Pericles amplifies his praise by saying that national character ensures Athenian military success. In contrast, our current president assured us that we could not expect victory in our present wars of counterinsurgency in traditional terms of meeting a defeated enemy head of state under formal terms of capitulation. Pericles, however, promises his audience that Athenians most certainly can win, if they, as in the past, continue to translate their civic liberality into military audacity and imagination.

In short, whereas the ancients saw value in popular culture translating into military efficacy, the modern mind less often makes the connection—even though the U.S. military is the world's preeminent force precisely because of its Periclean ability to channel American spontaneity, ingenuity, and free will into superior technological innovation, familiarity between the ranks, and creativity and ingenuity on the part of the officer corps in a way unknown by the old Soviet military, the regimented contemporary jihadist, or the rising Red Chinese army.

The traits that Pericles assumes as desirable—"refinement without extravagance," "knowledge without effeminacy," "wealth more for use than show," the disgrace of surrender to poverty, and politicians who are private citizens rather than professional officials—were, until recently, unquestioned American ideals. After all, most Americans privately concede that one should display wealth without being crass, that excessive intellectualism can lead to a less physical, less well-rounded life, that the poor are not always victims of uncontrolled circumstances, and that those successful in private enterprise are more likely to be so in public affairs. These are unfortunate realities that cannot easily be refuted except by the argument that it is hurtful to express publicly values that so many fail to aspire to. The difference, again, in the ancient and modern sentiment is that the latter worry whether such an expression will be deemed illiberal, and the former simply whether or not it is true.

In the most powerful section of the oration, Pericles proclaims that Athenian culture and politics have created a unique individual who is multi-talented and innately magnanimous, given both the plentitude at his disposal and his innately liberal character. In sum, Pericles first introduces the now stereotyped portrait of the well-rounded thinker and fighter, who is more courageous precisely because he is both well apprised of the danger he so willingly confronts, and has so much more to lose than his regimented enemies who only face the dangers of war through coercion or desperation.

Here, Pericles has touched upon an eternal paradox of democratic societies in wartime. Nothing has proved more moving and heart-rending in our contemporary conflicts than middle-class American suburbanites of the luxurious postmodern world willingly, eagerly, and superbly battling jihadists of the premodern landscape, whether in the Hindu Kush or Anbar Province. We can locate the recklessness of the suicide bomber in part in fanatical religious observance, and in part in the desperation arising from the misery of his material existence. But how, other than through Periclean democratic courage, do we explain why the upscale American, with so much to lose, has so often proved his enemy's superior not just in battle competency, but in will power as well? Or as Pericles sums up: "The palm of courage will surely be adjudged most justly to those who best know the difference between hardship and pleasure and yet are never tempted to shrink from danger."

The most famous line in the Funeral Speech is a triumphalist assertion:

> I say that as a city we are the school of Hellas, while I doubt if the world can produce a man who, where he has only himself to depend upon, is equal to so many emergencies, and graced by so happy a versatility, as the Athenian.

Similar chest-thumping American braggadocio disappeared with the conclusion of World War II. Yet if one were to consider dispassionately the global presence of American military officers, professors, engineers, corporate CEOs, missionaries, aid workers, diplomats, and tourists, there is nothing quite comparable to the versatile and ubiquitous American.

Pericles then immediately supports this "no mere boast" by the additional proof that (a) the city's defeated enemies typically accept that they were beaten by a superior foe, (b) those ruled by Athens acknowledge their master's power, (c) Athenians are omnipresent abroad, "having forced every sea and land to be the highway of our daring," and (d) they "have left imperishable monuments behind us."

An American Pericles would have to remind his countrymen that one mark of our power is our defeated enemies' boast that they have given us a good fight; that the defeated Japanese or Germans now acknowledge that they were lucky to have fallen within our postwar proconsulship; that the seas everywhere today, from the Aegean to the Persian Gulf, are home to American ships; and that such ubiquity is both essential to our national security and a benefit to the global order as well. Moreover, generations of Americans have left imperishable monuments of their civilization's power and morality behind them. That latter fact I can personally attest to as a former member of the American Battle Monuments Commission that oversees twenty-four American cemeteries on foreign soil, from North Africa to Mexico City to the Pacific to Europe, and cares for another twenty-five battle monuments abroad.

Pericles' point in reciting the past courage, skill, and sacrifice of ancestral Athenians is to urge his beleaguered and wearied audience that "every one of their survivors be ready to suffer in her cause." He offers a final reminder, that "our stake in the struggle is not the same as theirs who have no such blessings to lose." Again, Pericles struggles with the undeniable premodern/postmodern paradox that confronts all members of affluent and free societies: only sacrifice and singular courage in the past created unmatched present bounty, yet social and economic success make life so enjoyable—and precious—that it is hard to ask anyone to risk giving it up, especially in the salad days of youth. But such sacrifice is at times necessary, especially if deemed improbable by opportunistic enemies with far less to lose and far more to gain.

In his peroration, Pericles turns from Athenian exempla to a more universal lesson about human nature and its expression in times of ultimate sacrifice during war—a tutorial that my father once instilled in me at an unthinking and self-indulgent young age:

For there is justice in the claim that steadfastness in his country's battles should be as a cloak to cover a man's other imperfections; since the good action has blotted out the bad, and his merit as a citizen more than outweighed his demerits as an individual. But none of these allowed either wealth with its prospect of future enjoyment to unnerve his spirit, or poverty with its hope of a day of freedom and riches to tempt him to shrink from danger.

Pericles does not mean that the felon is pardoned from society's wrath because he was once a hoplite steadfast in battle; rather, past service warrants some weight in any overall assessment of a citizen's character. In other words, society must collectively offer some exemption to the loud plumber who drinks too much, the lawyer who dresses sloppily, the thrice-divorced doctor, or the so-so C– student should they have, at one time in their lives, risked their all on the field of battle for their compatriots back home. What makes some Athenians or Americans successful in calm does not ensure that they will be in war, just as the veteran might find that his martial virtues do not translate into a happy life during the tranquility of peace.

At the age of twelve, I once laughed at a strange junkman, overweight, smoking, and loud, asking for my father, who drove in our yard. Almost immediately, I was nearly shaken out of my senses by an enraged father, who sat me down and lectured for twenty minutes that Mr. X, as a daring and brilliant bomber pilot, had, just twenty years earlier, flown him and ten others on forty successful B-29 missions, saved his crew from certain annihilation on two occasions, landed under impossible emergency conditions three times on Iwo Jima, and then volunteered five years later to fly more than fifty missions over Korea amid enemy jet fighters. Or as my father concluded—and I can still hear his thundering words as if he delivered that terrifying sermon yesterday—"Sometimes what makes a man the best in war makes him not so lucky in peace." I think now that he, like Pericles, was trying to warn me that no matter what his pilot did for the rest of his life, my father would interpret it against a backdrop of thanks for his wartime courage and competency on behalf of all of us.

Of course, Pericles does not make only rational arguments to bolster his demoralized Athenians. The Funeral Oration is also justly famous also for its emotive quality, its beautiful entreaty not just to seek honor, but indeed to love Athens:

> You must yourselves realize the power of Athens, and feed your eyes upon her from day to day, till love of her fills your hearts; and then, when all her greatness shall break upon you, you must reflect that it was by courage, sense of duty, and a keen feeling of honor in action that men were enabled to win all this, and that no personal failure in an enterprise could make them consent to deprive their country of their valour, but they laid it at her feet as the most glorious contribution that they could offer. . . . For heroes have the whole earth for their tomb; and in lands far from their own, where the column with its epitaph declares it, there is enshrined in every breast a record unwritten with no tablet to preserve it, except that of the heart.

Our leaders often list American virtues, and note American successes, but they rarely remind our citizens that American accomplishment and values might lead to a sort of love of America. Millions of Americans, of course, feel for the United States what Pericles felt toward his polis, but rarely are we reminded of the transcendent beauty of American culture that so protects the individual and makes him a fortunate part of what most others on the planet aspire to. When we list the rogues' gallery of thugs and killers that the United States has gone to war against in the last three generations—Hitler, Mussolini, Tojo, Kim il-Sung, Ho Chi Minh, the Stalinists, Manuel Noriega, Saddam Hussein, the Taliban, Osama bin Laden—while providing postwar aid rather than annexing conquered land, it reminds us that no other country has had either the capability or willingness to take on such burdens.

Pericles concludes with a reminder that it is neither riches nor material acquisition that stays with us to the end, but only honor—which derives from protecting the polis and fulfilling our civic obligations in its time of need: "For it is only the love of honor that never grows old; and honor it is, not gain, as some would have it, that rejoices the heart of age and helplessness."

Of course, between Pericles and us moderns lies the abyss of industrialized warfare. At Verdun, at the Somme, or at Stalingrad, honor seemed to be overshadowed by grotesque barbarism and false calls of idealism. Nonetheless, honor is not a calcified twentieth-century concept, but, as Pericles reminds us, a value that does not grow old across time and space. Behind George Bush's order for a surge into Anbar Province at a time when most had written off the idea of a free and democratic Iraq and behind the decision of Barack Obama to send Navy SEALs into Pakistan to kill the mass-murdering bin Laden was the idea, even if unexpressed, of honor—the notion of America's collective good name, which we sought not to tarnish by allowing our enemies to defeat our cause and in the Homeric sense claim that they were our betters. That idea of ancient *timê* is now the objective of vituperations on the rare occasions it is invoked, yet is almost innately recognized and lauded when it reappears.

Contemporary critics see in the Funeral Oration mostly misplaced imperialism, along with underlying sexism, xenophobia, militarism, and cultural triumphalism. There surely are elements of each present in the speech. But it is not in this critical spirit that millions still read the oration in Thucydides' history nearly 2,500 years after Pericles delivered a version of it. For the classical Greeks, Periclean candor was not predicated on whether it would be wise, politically sensitive, or hurtful, but whether the message was found to be true. Most of what Pericles said to his audience was not only representative of the Athenian experience, but also a fair assessment of human nature transcending democratic values.

The real lesson of the Periclean Oration is not merely that some Athenian values should be our own, but that in our place, according to our station, we too might have the imagination to articulate the singularity of our culture and the bravery to proclaim it without apology or qualification. To do otherwise, is to enjoy the unmatched bounty and freedom of the United States without gratitude to those of the past who bequeathed it, and without present awareness that what we enjoy makes us blessed beyond the comprehension of most of the six billion others on the planet.

In short, Pericles reminds Americans that, should a great culture not feel that its values and achievements are exceptional, then few others will as well—a fact injurious to a small and insignificant state, but fatal for a power with aspirations of global leadership. A leader who relentlessly reminds his countrymen of their shortcomings will naturally apologize abroad for them as well, and what starts as self-critique becomes a self-fulfilling prophecy of national decline.

A Prometheus Bound

Andrew Roberts

LIKE THE ROMAN, contemplating the Huns amassing north of the Rubicon in the late fourth century A.D., or an Englishman surveying the demise of the British Empire in Asia in the 1940s, today's perceptive American might be forgiven for viewing his country's future with a deep sense of foreboding, and concluding that the days of the United States' global *imperium* are numbered. No great insight is needed to read the runes; they are evident with every flicker of the 24/7 news cycle. The precise pathology of America's largely self-ordained retreat from hegemony can be left to the historians: what should concern us now is whether the post-American world will be any better, or will it be the presage for a new Dark Age for mankind?

Quite why the American nation permitted itself in the last decades of the twentieth and opening ones of the twenty-first centuries to shed its traditional, muscular, and distinctive—indeed exceptional—cultural and political identity, in order to embrace an effete European-style social democracy, must also be left to historians. For just as the Europeans were proving themselves incapable of even reproduction and were taking on wildly unsustainable levels of public debt in countries such as Greece,

Portugal, Spain, and Italy, the United States began emulating them, even embarking on that most ruinous of all European social adventures: nationalized medicine. A society already threatened by hypochondria, obesity, and litigiousness thus busily stoked up its own funeral pyre.

In the year 2011 alone, the United States had to watch China overtake her in manufacturing output by value, ending over a century of American primacy in this vital area. She was forced to watch passively as China launched its first aircraft carriers of many planned. The fleet will one day wrest the balance of power in the South China Sea from the United States and her Asian allies. She has chosen to loiter on the sidelines while Colonel Gaddafi, the man who murdered 270 Americans and Britons in cold blood over Lockerbie, continued successfully to defy NATO for five months (and counting). Meanwhile, the nation that prides itself in having been born in a revolution for liberty has confined herself to bleating inconsequential, belated weasel words of worthless support for peoples fighting desperately for freedom during the Arab Spring, ensuring that the dictators who are so far surviving are the most ruthless and most anti-American ones.

Perhaps worst of all, at least for 2011, the United States has been told by a leading credit agency that her paper is no longer to be fully trusted in the markets of the world—that her promise that she will repay her debts cannot be wholly believed. Standard & Poor's reassuringly boring CEO, John Chambers, took to the television screens and effectively said that America was no longer quite 100 percent trustworthy when it came to money, and the markets emphatically believed him rather than the protestations of the chief executive of the United States and his Treasury Secretary. This was a straightforward moral issue: America was being accused of being so irresponsibly spendthrift that she came within hours of defaulting on her loans—yet it was merely treated as a financial issue, another sign of societal degeneracy. The United States has been told that her word of honor now trades at a discount, for the first time since credit rating was invented seventy years ago. Small wonder that only 10 percent of Americans regard their Congress in a positive light; the only question remaining must be: who on earth are those 10 percent?

It was *not* ever thus. Not so long ago, America was a country that protected her friends and chastised her enemies. In finance, her word was quite literally her bond. Her Congress was respected throughout the world, not least for its sturdy patriotism. She genuinely believed that her best days were ahead of her, and did not fear—as Americans must today—that that was merely a politician's cheesy applause line. Americans did not need to be told by her president that theirs was "a triple-A country," since no-one suspected otherwise. She was proud of her exceptionalism, born of an identity that was not wracked with guilt about being a superpower, but was rightly jealous and suspicious of any state that aspired to supplant her, especially those that did not espouse her message of liberty. The Pax Americana was just that: a system underwritten by America that guaranteed peace between the powers, rather than the fragile arrangement that we see today, where the State Department pleads with states such as Iran and North Korea not to upset the nuclear balance. America as supplicant is a dispiriting—not to say revolting—sight, but one we had all better get used to.

And for what end has the United States sacrificed that civilizational vitality that made her so exceptional in the century since Teddy Roosevelt waved farewell to the Great White Fleet in February 1909, as it steamed off from the Hampton Roads, Virginia, for its circumnavigation of the planet, telling the world that America had arrived on the scene as a Great Power to be reckoned with? Has America been defeated in a great war, going down fighting "for the ashes of his father and the temple of his gods," like Horatius on the bridge? Has the United States sacrificed its global primacy because it was too busy curing cancer, ending world poverty, or ushering in a nirvana of world peace? The Roman Empire fell for a number of reasons, but only after six centuries as top-dog world power. The British Empire was the only force to fight from the beginning of the war all the way through to its end, and after the Fall of France it was the only entity at war with Nazi Germany until Hitler's invasion of Russia a year later. The American hegemony, by contrast, seems about to sacrifice itself not in mankind's noblest causes, but as the result of chronic overspending on Medicare, Medicaid, and unaffordable social programs. Where is the everlasting, untarnishable glory in that?

Of course, America is not about to leave the top table of world powers any time soon. It is still far the strongest military power, although it will most probably cede its position as the strongest economic power to China before the end of the current decade. Its voice will continue to carry weight in the councils of the world, though less as the years pass. Its universities—or at least those parts of them unaffected by the left's long march through their humanities departments—will still be the best in the world. Its most innovative companies, such as Google, Apple, and Boeing, will still stand as beacons to the rest of capitalist enterprise. Yet for all those substantial consolation prizes, the United States will have lost its primacy, its commanding voice, its edge. It will be just another successful, rich country, another Germany or Japan, except bigger. It will have shrunk from the world leader that effectively decided the fate of our planet to yet one more player in the post-American world. When that happens, the West shall have lost something inestimable, and civilization something irreplaceable. For when America is no longer exceptional, we shall all—Americans and non-Americans alike—be the losers.

Hard-wired into America's DNA is an idealism, a faith, and a sense of decency and generosity that it is utterly impossible to detect in any of its likely successor powers. The Enlightenment concepts that inspired its Founding Fathers placed liberty far higher on their list of non-negotiable demands than would have been the case even a few decades earlier, or, one suspects, much later. When the French Revolution broke out, less than a decade after America finally won its eight-year War of Independence, liberty was only given a billing alongside with equality and fraternity in the list of the Jacobins' desiderata. (In my youth I recall a *Spectator* cartoon of an orator crying, "Liberty! Equality! Fraternity!" only for a heckler from the crowd to shout back: "Well make your mind up!") As the French, Russian, Chinese, Vietnamese, Cuban, and any number of other revolutions have conclusively proved, one simply cannot have liberty, equality, *and* fraternity in any society, because each is fundamentally opposed to the other two. The genius of the Founding Fathers was to appreciate this, indeed to embrace it by raising liberty so high in the Constitution of 1787 that it emerged to the overt detriment of both equality and fraternity. (No framers who believed in fraternity would have introduced quite so many checks and balances into their founding documents.)

The lack of any provisions for establishing financial equality in the Constitution, either of opportunity or outcome, was undoubtedly one of its strengths, allowing for a free-market capitalism to thrive that soon made the United States the most powerful economy on earth. Of course, it also left the slaves unemancipated in 1776, but even there one sees, four score and seven years later, an astonishing willingness of Americans to sacrifice themselves for an ideal. For 364,500 Union soldiers to give their lives in the Civil War, in a American population of only 31.4 million, shows the lengths to which ordinary Americans were willing to go in order to abolish slavery. I doubt whether Britain would have abolished slavery in 1807 had she known the price would be that high.

With slavery abolished at home, every generation since the Civil War has seen Americans go far beyond the call to duty to see liberty prevail abroad. It is this kind of self-sacrifice that will certainly be lost to international relations once China, India, or whatever international cartel-alliance replaces the United States as global bigwig and gets the whip hand. After the Spanish-American War, the United States brought peace, order, and good government to huge swathes of the world previously ruled cruelly, corruptly, and inefficiently by Spain. Today, schoolchildren are taught about the negative aspects of American rule in the Philippines and the rest of the former Spanish Empire, but overall the inhabitants of each of those places saw a standard of living undreamed of in any other empire besides the British.

America sent out her brightest and best to administer these territories, and they did their country proud. George Santayana described the British imperialists as "boyish masters," and the same can be said for the Americans after 1898. Theodore Roosevelt's aid to Panama, which helped to establish its independence from Colombia, as well as America's many interventions in Latin

America in the first two decades of the twentieth century, have long been held up by the anti-American left as being primarily motivated by strategic and economic best interests, without the necessary extrapolations being followed up, which is that a healthy American economy was a prerequisite for successful local development in the rest of Latin America. The Panama Canal has brought more prosperity to the Caribbean than any number of other costly, taxpayer-funded development programs.

The United States had no vital national interest in entering the Great War in 1917, yet so outraged was she by imperial Germany's brutal adoption of unrestricted submarine warfare, coming on top of other barbarities, such as the sinking of the *Lusitania* and insults such as the Zimmerman Telegram, that even the naturally pacific Woodrow Wilson was induced to declare war. Although Wilson can be accused of naïveté in the redrawing of European and Middle Eastern frontiers at the Versailles Conference and afterwards, it was at least in sharp contrast to the cynicism, greed, and desire for vengeance exhibited by European statesmen such as David Lloyd George and Georges Clemenceau. The concept of national self-determination of peoples led to further complications, but it was at least an idealistic attempt to extend freedom and independence to ethnic groupings of the European continent, which had experienced precious little of either for centuries. Moreover, the United States gained nothing by its mediation; Wilson was indeed an honest broker, even if some of the hyphenated countries his policy brought into being—notably Czecho-Slovakia and Yugo-Slavia—had unhappy subsequent histories.

Similarly, although it was Adolf Hitler who declared war on the United States on December 11, 1941, and not the other way around, the decision by the Roosevelt

Administration to adopt a "Germany First" policy was the most statesmanlike single decision of the twentieth century. Despite the fact that America had been attacked in the Pacific, within a year U.S. forces had landed a quarter of a million men on the coast of northwest Africa in Operation Torch. The notion was that it was vital for the United States to knock out its strongest antagonist first. With truly Themistoclean foresight, President Franklin Roosevelt, Army Chief of Staff General George C. Marshall, Joint Chiefs Chairman Admiral William Leahy, and their key planner Brigadier General Dwight D. Eisenhower ignored the cries for immediate revenge against the Japanese for Pearl Harbor and instead concentrated on destroying Nazi Germany, channeling over 70 percent of the war effort to the Western theaters. It was a winning strategy.

How easy it would have been for the White House and War Department to have bowed to the calls of Press and Congress to adopt a Pacific First policy and smite Japan early while leaving Germany until later. Had that happened there is no knowing what might have happened in the West in the meantime, with either Hitler or Stalin likely to have been in complete control of the continent from Brest to the Urals by 1946 or 1947. Once again, American selflessness in foreign policy redounded to the benefit of mankind in extirpating Fascism. As in the Great War, America left the Second World War with no territorial aggrandizement to its name, despite its possession of the world's only nuclear weaponry. Such self-abnegation at the end of a vast conflict is unknown to human history, yet few have given the United States any credit for it.

For all that left-wing and revisionist historians have tried to blame the United States for starting the Cold War, in fact it was Stalin who made it clear that the entire world would be the new theater for a titanic clash between Communism and Capitalism, almost as soon as World War II ended. By the time that Winston Churchill delivered his "Iron Curtain" speech in March 1946—tellingly in America rather than Europe because he wanted to awaken Americans to the new threat—Stalin had already made it clear that he was going to take all of Eastern Europe into the Soviet maw, despite the assurances regarding the "independence and integrity" of those countries that he had given at Yalta. It is often forgotten that Churchill's message was not well received in the United States, even by President Truman who was sitting next to him on the podium when it was delivered, because Americans still wished to believe the best of their brave wartime ally, the Soviet Union. It took Churchill's great speech and the Berlin blockade and subsequent airlift two years later to wake Americans up to the fact that a Cold War had been silently declared against them, and that they needed to gird themselves to a totally different kind of conflict.

Yet Americans did not need to fight the Cold War if they didn't want to. What, ultimately, did it matter to them if faraway countries with which they did little trade, such as Korea or Vietnam, went Communist? An isolationist Fortress America, trading with Europe, the Americas, Australasia, Africa, and the Middle East from an economic base far stronger than Russia's could easily have left countries on the other side of the Pacific fall prey to totalitarianism if it had so chosen. America could have looked the other way as freedom was crushed, as France and Britain had done with Czechoslovakia in 1938. It was always a perfectly viable option for the Truman, Eisenhower, Kennedy, Johnson, and Nixon Administrations, yet none of them adopted it. This was not out of a spirit of cowboy-like aggression (which is the left's analysis) but because, as JFK articulated in his inauguration address, the United States was genuinely prepared to "pay any price, bear any burden, meet any hardship, support any friend, oppose any foe, to assure the survival and the success of liberty." The price was never less than enormous: over four years after June 1947, the Marshall Plan directed $13 billion in aid to modernize Europe and make it prosperous again, as a means of saving the western part of the continent from Communism. (Needless to say, the left merely portray this as a selfish move to try to create export markets for American goods.)

Of course inaugural addresses must, along with lapidary inscriptions, budget forecasts, and lovers' oaths, be treated with a degree of healthy scepticism. Yet, in this case, the 53,000 Americans killed in Korea, 58,000 in Vietnam, and 5,706 (and counting) in the War on Terror, as well as others in places like Somalia, Beirut, and the First Gulf War, do substantiate JFK's words. There were no American interests at stake in Bosnia in the 1990s, for example, yet Americans still died there to extend freedom. Recently this idealism has been denounced as "neoconservatism," but at the time of JFK's inaugural it was more properly recognized as America's great gift to mankind. (The Republican presidential candidates who today almost uniformly denounce American involvement in Libya, on the grounds that there are no American national interests involved, would do well to recall that NATO sent troops to Afghanistan in 2001, despite few Europeans dying on 9/11.)

America's belief in the universal benefit of liberty was a gift to mankind entirely born of American exceptionalism. Other, earlier empires—the British Empire included—did not consider it to be their duty to right the world's wrongs globally. Ancient Rome only went to places where it thought it could extract tribute, raw materials, or profits, and it certainly never went anywhere in order to make the lives of the locals better—ditto the latter-day empires of France, Spain, Germany, and especially Belgium. Britain's George Canning did help the liberation movements in Latin America in the first two decades of the nineteenth century, and Britain protected Portugal with military interventions, but in general she concentrated only on those parts of the world where British subjects needed support; with the Royal Navy unable to proceed far inland, these tended to be in coastal areas.

Those great infrastructure projects that Britain did bequeath to her Empire—railways, telegraphs, irrigation systems, canals, clinics, universities, ports, New Delhi, and so on—generally saw economic, cultural, and military benefits. There was precious little of the sheer philanthropic generosity (for no realpolitik return) that one saw in the Bush Administration's outlay of $15 billion to fight AIDS in Africa, for example.

One of the things that makes America exceptional, at least when it is remaining true to itself and not suffering from its present case of severe personality disorder, is the universalism of its creed of liberty. There is no universalism in the title deeds of British liberty, which pertain only to British subjects rather than to non-Britons, let alone to anyone wanting to enjoy "life, liberty and the pursuit of happiness." That universalism, that belief that the liberties guaranteed by democracy and the Constitution are a magnificent gift that should be extended throughout the globe, is peculiar to the United States. It is the reason that Margaret Thatcher stated: "In my lifetime I have seen all the problems coming from Europe, and the solutions coming from America."

For all the declarations that the United Nations might make on the subject, there are really no such things as basic human rights—i.e., legally enforceable rights that devolve upon everyone born on Planet Earth, simply because they are human. The only meaningful rights are derived from the declarations by nations themselves—the 1689 Bill of Rights in Britain or the 1791 Bill of Rights in America—not from multinational bodies with no police forces, such as the United Nations or the European Union, merely stating that rights exist, and then doing nothing to substantiate them. True liberty stems from the ancient founding documents of Western democracy, as debated and voted upon by representative institutions, rather than from the theoretical spoutings of multilateral bodies with no vital interest in the outcome or ability to enforce such utopianism.

In losing faith in her exceptionalism, in succumbing to a Europeanization of her polity, and in falling into $3 trillion of debt to a rival and Communist government, America is simply not being herself. She has taken on a different personality, one that is profoundly antipathetic to the values and traditions that made her great. Instead of continuing the adventurous traditions of the Pilgrims, the genius of the Founding Fathers, the devil-take-the-hindmost enterprise of the nineteenth-century tamers of the Wild West, and the courage of the Greatest Generation, modern America—once a Prometheus—has allowed herself to be restrained and bowed by those who ultimately do not wish her well. Regulatory authorities, the teachers' trade unions, the United Nations, political correctness, welfare dependency, the human rights industry, postmodernist intellectuals, a malicious media, Ivy League humanities departments, Hollywood pieties, ultra-permissiveness,

New Age drivel: all these and many more bind the American Prometheus, and lacerate it in the process.

Today there are no fewer than 216 departments of peace studies at American institutions of higher education, but only four departments of strategy (i.e. war) studies. When Barney Frank on the left and Ron Paul on the libertarian right come together to criticize "militarism" and NATO, and to tell the American people that they can't afford to be the "world's policeman" any more, they are preaching much the same gospel as that enunciated by Charles Lindbergh in the 1930s, shorn of the anti-Semitism. Yet their call to dismantle down the Pax Americana established by Truman over sixty years ago is falling on willing ears only because of a ceaseless campaign by those who refuse to accept the concept of American chivalry.

The role of the public intellectual in undermining American self-confidence at home and abroad cannot be overestimated. Nothing has been more damaging to civilizational vitality than their constant sniping criticism, from the days of Vietnam and Watergate onwards, of American actions abroad. (It is interesting how often denunciations of American cultural imperialism emanate from Western intellectuals wearing Levi jeans who get coffee at Starbucks while listening to Bruce Springsteen on their Apple iPods.) We are all familiar with the concept of self-hating Jews, but it is self-hating Americans—mainly on the left, but one occasionally sees it on the right too—who undermine the United States with their automatic assumption that anything America does abroad will be for the worse, especially in the military sphere.

One does not need to go to the works of Noam Chomsky to see this effect. Charles Jencks, the American landform artist, told BBC Radio 4's "Start the Week" program on May 30 this year about the time when he was asked to design a garden in Paris in 2003. "I naturally took war and chaos," as his theme, he said, and "used it to signify the Israeli-Palestinian tit-for-tat, when Iraq was being invaded with this pseudo War on Terror." Jencks added that he likes to work with scientists in creating what he calls "metaphysical landscapes" but says that they are "victims often of metaphors which are third hand ... retrogressive metaphors like Big Bang, which is basically a Bush/Joint Chiefs of Staff metaphor." When even uppity gardeners think that scientific expressions such as the Big Bang Theory, which has been in common scientific parlance since Edouard Lemaître proposed it in the 1920s, long before President George W. Bush was born, is "basically a Bush/Joint Chiefs of Staff metaphor," we really have reached a low-point in our foreign policy discourse. (By the way, if one wants to encounter something genuinely "pseudo," forget the War on Terror, and instead look at Jencks's 2007 book *Critical Modernism: Where is Post Modernism Going?*, a masterpiece of pseudo-intellectuality.)

The ultimate intention of the intellectuals' critique of American traditions, values, history, customs, and assumptions is to undermine America's pride in herself, especially in her exceptionalism. The Italian Marxist writer Antonio Gramsci preached that the bourgeois cultural hegemony could only be destroyed by unceasing cultural warfare principally conducted in the media and the academy, and his many disciples have taken his teaching to heart, particularly in their assault on American exceptionalism. Manifest Destiny was always a fiction, of course—nothing in human affairs is manifest—but it was a noble and unifying national fiction. Nations need romance and myths, for without them, as Edmund Burke warned in *Reflections on the Revolution in France,* the "age of chivalry is gone.

That of sophisters, economists, and calculators, has succeeded."

Fortunately, American culture is infused with highly romantic myths, fictions, dreams, phantasms, and ideals, which keep her vibrant, confident, chivalrous, and exceptional. The stories of Omaha Beach; of the Wild West; of Mr. Smith going to Washington; of the Frontiersman; of the huddled masses who work hard and ultimately succeed; of the Alamo; of the victim of persecution who can finally speak truth to power; of Custer's Last Stand; of George Washington who couldn't tell a lie; of the farmer in the Norman Rockwell painting exercising his freedom of speech at a town hall meeting; of the "Spirit of '76"; of the rail-splitting president brought up in a one-room log cabin; of the writer in the garret who pens the Great American Novel; of how any child can grow up to be president; of the winter at Valley Forge; of the shining city on the hill; of the defense of Guadalcanal and Bastogne; of Paul Revere's ride: these are only a few of the truths, tales, myths, and ideals to which America needs to return in order to regain her exceptionalism, even in the face of the sneers of the intellectuals and the jibes of the late-night satire shows.

Why should it be such a leap of faith to believe in these building blocks of American identity, considering what Protestants are required to believe about the Resurrection, Catholics about transubstantiation, Buddhists about reincarnation, Jews about the parting of the Red Sea, and so on? American Dreams have traditionally been sources of abiding strength to the people of the United States in the past. They have been dangerously neglected in recent years, as those Santayana called the "scientific blackguards, conspirators, churls, and fanatics" have imposed their rancidly literal or revisionist interpretations instead.

The demonization of the rich and successful is a very dangerous cultural development for any society, and a potentially suicidal one for a country such as the United States, where the free market used to be part of the national raison d'etre. Disparities between rich and poor might be greater in the United States than in Europe and especially in confiscatorily taxed Scandinavia, but they are mild compared to most of Africa, Asia, Russia, Latin America, and the Middle East. Yet the level of resentment against the rich in America—as exemplified by President Obama's mantra criticizing the "millionaires and the billionaires"—is monstrous in a society that so completely depends on its wealth creators.

The only people whom the media seem to think deserve high pay are actors and sportsmen, rather than anyone who actually provides employment for others. When I took my children to see the feature-length cartoon *Cars 2* recently, I knew immediately that the villain would eventually turn out to be Miles Axelrod, despite his being introduced in laudatory terms as an environmentally friendly researcher into alternative fuels, because he was described as a self-made billionaire. In popular entertainment, wealth is increasingly seen as synonymous with malfeasance. Of course, the apotheosis of the politics of envy, class warfare, and social resentment could be seen in my home city of London over four days in August 2011, when feral raptors looted every business in their path (except bookshops).

In the "Schadengasm" of delight from the left over the travails of News Corporation regarding the phone hacking scandal, the wealth of Rupert Murdoch was deployed against him almost as unanswerable evidence of wrongdoing, despite the fact that the *News of the World* represented only 1 percent of his business, and the wrongdoers could probably be counted on the fingers of one hand, out of his 53,000 employees. Wealth creators, business builders, employers, profit-winners, exporters, the people who contribute the taxes that pay for colleges and clinics: these are the people whom Americans should honor, admire, and seek to emulate. They used to when Benjamin Franklin and, later, Samuel Smiles wrote their classic self-help books of the eighteenth and nineteenth centuries, but that has all been lost in a welter of envy politics and worship of the worthless. (Of course in the postmodernist lexicon, nothing can be denounced as worthless, just as the gangsta rapper cannot be said to be a better or worse musician than Beethoven.)

In 2008 the Indian intellectual and CNN talk show host Fareed Zakaria published a book titled *The Post-American World,* which pointed out that the "tallest buildings, biggest dams, top-selling movies and most advanced mobile phones are all being built or made outside the United States," and concluded that, in this "new world," the United States was definitely a losing rather than a winning nation, that the "central role of the United States will inevitably shrink." Zakaria believes that in this new world America must "move from being the dominating hegemon to a role more like an honest broker." It is true that no nation has been more honest over the past two centuries, and with its present debt ceiling being raised to over $16 trillion no nation could be broker, but will ordinary Americans go along with this counsel of despair? Amongst the many incongruous sights that Alexis de Tocqueville witnessed during the 1848 revolution in Paris was a politician sprinting down the street after a crowd. "I am their leader!" he shouted to Tocqueville. "I must follow them!" The present American political leadership in the White House, Senate, and House of Representatives are adopting his ungainly posture, and they are understandably incurring odium as a result.

At least during the 1848 revolutions politicians still employed great oratory in order to persuade. It is astonishing that President Obama, whose election campaign saw a series of rhetorical extravaganzas, has not delivered a single truly great speech since his inauguration. Historians will debate the lowest point when it comes to stomach-churning presidential schmaltz, but my favorite moment came on January 12, 2011 when he attended a memorial service for the victims of the Tucson shootings, and said of one of them, a nine-year-old girl: "If there are rain puddles in heaven, Christina is jumping in them today."

Great oratory or no, Zakaria's post-American world is on its way, and the witness of history is that once great nations start to unravel they tend to do it faster than anyone originally expected. Perhaps the point has already been reached where globalization has made American relative decline irreversible vis à vis China, India, Brazil, Russia, South Africa, and so on. Maybe what Teddy Roosevelt would have thought of as the "burdens of empire," what Eisenhower, JFK, Nixon, and Reagan thought of as the responsibilities of a superpower in upholding liberty against an Evil Empire, and what George W. Bush rightly termed the "Long War" against Islamofascism, are now simply beyond a bowed and overextended America. Is this the decade when the United States steps away from her historic, self-imposed duty to protect and if possible extend democracy and the boundaries of the free world?

As the hymnal reminds us, "Earth's proud empires pass away," and of course in the fullness of time America's *imperium* must pass, too. But anyone in the West—indeed, pretty much anyone outside Beijing's Forbidden

City—who actively looks forward to that day should think again. America has discharged her world-historical obligations to the West and to civilization in an utterly exemplary fashion over the past century. Under absolutely no invasion threat herself whatsoever from anyone in well over a century, she has sent her young men to fight against totalitarianism time after time, sometimes at terrible cost. Mostly she has won; on one occasion—in Vietnam—she was defeated, though largely because of pacifism at home rather than military defeat in the field. She could have behaved with the realpolitik and selfishness of earlier empires, but instead chose to help those beyond her borders struggling to be free.

The United States spent untold billions becoming the arsenal of democracy in the war against fascism, helping the Soviet Union in its war against the Nazis, bombing German war production factories, invading North Africa, Sicily, Italy, Northern France, and eventually Germany itself, despite never coming under any threat from the Nazis herself. She then never flinched in the Cold War against Soviet Communism, even when the Cuban Missile Crisis threatened her own annihilation. Under George W. Bush she again had recourse to bring free and representative institutions to a country hitherto ruled by one of history's most evil dictators, and also to evict the vicious Taliban from the government of Afghanistan. Despite its being denounced at the time by the antiwar movement as "illegal," the War against Terror has been prosecuted by Barack Obama, complete with a "surge" and the continued use of Guantánamo Bay.

Compared to America's record of selfless support for democracy and representative institutions all around the world for over a century, we see in the rise of China a rival to the United States whose ruthlessness, militarism, contempt for freedom of speech, saber-rattling towards its neighbors, brutality towards its own people, profound dishonesty about its society, and cyberwarfare against Western governments, institutions, and companies make it a dangerous adversary. By unleashing the genius of the Chinese people for hard work and enterprise, China's nominally Marxist leaders hope to defeat the capitalists at their own game and then bury them. Resentful after centuries of perceived exploitation by the West, the small Communist Party clique that rules China—a *nomenklatura* that is in many cases descended from the original revolutionaries of the 1930s and 1940s—looks forward to the vengeance it will wreak, slowly and by drips. I do not envy the world my children will have to live in should they succeed.

America is still the last great hope of mankind, although far too few Americans appreciate this, and those who do can't easily see how to continue turning that hope into a reality. "How do you make children patriotic?" Winston Churchill once rhetorically asked his education secretary Rab Butler, before answering himself: "Tell them Wolfe took Quebec." From the crowds chanting "USA! USA!" at the Phillies' baseball stadium when the news was announced of the killing of Osama bin Laden, there is perhaps hope for a renaissance of American pride in time to protect mankind from that ultimate dystopia: a post-American world. A return to the values of the real America—rather than Mr. Obama's ersatz Europeanized version—is the best prescription, but time is running out. America must escape her nemesis, not just for herself but for the sake of civilization.

America & the Angels of Sacré-Cœur

David Bentley Hart

I will pour out my spirit upon all flesh; and your sons and your daughters shall prophesy, your old men shall dream dreams, your young men shall see visions . . .

—Joel 2:28

FROM THE OUTSIDE, Montmartre's Sacré-Cœur Basilica presents something of an aesthetic problem. It is a striking edifice, needless to say, soaring up as it does at the very summit of Paris, a bright white riot of demi-ovate domes and cupolas, elongated arches, and intrepidly clashing decorative motifs. But it is also very much a product of its time, with a little too much *fin de siècle* preciosity about it. If one views its alleged fusion of Romanesque and Byzantine styles at a sardonic slant, it can look suspiciously like a meretricious pastiche, full of late Romantic medievalist and orientalist clichés. Contemplated at a distance, under the Parisian sky, it all sometimes seems not so much an organic expression of the spiritual aspirations of French culture as a patently synthetic memorial to them, concocted from equal parts morbid nostalgia and sugary fantasy.

On the inside, however, it is very different: more austere, more a matter of softly golden stone and muted sunlight.

There is, admittedly, that huge, hideous mosaic from the 1920s in the apse (a titanic Christ with a gilded heart, flanked by the lesser colossi of the Blessed Virgin and St. Michael, all three towering over a scampering horde of mitered and haloed imps), but otherwise the interior is genuinely, if somberly, beautiful. And one feature of the vault can produce an effect that is truly sublime. There are four large stone angels with outspread wings, carved in relief, one each, in the pendentives below the central dome. When one enters the basilica out of bright daylight, however, they are not immediately visible, but remain hidden in the shadows below the ring of windows at the dome's base. It is only as one's eyes adjust to the light that they emerge, all at once, from the darkness. If one is unprepared for it, it is a startling experience, even slightly terrifying; for just a few seconds, one senses the advent— and the gaze—of immense and numinous presences.

At that moment, any lingering aesthetic reservations can be set aside. However dubious certain features of its design may be, there can be no doubt just then that Sacré-Cœur does authentically express something of the genius of French Christian tradition. Ultimately, it is all a question of causality. Obviously, those angels looming so magnificently overhead are there as a result of the material and efficient causes that went into the building's planning and construction: Travertine limestone, bricks, sculptors, Paul Abadie, money, the political tensions of the Third Republic, and so on. But, in another sense, it was the angels who summoned the basilica into being; they provided the final and formal causes that raised it up out of the substrate of mere unformed matter. Were it not for the transcendent longings they embodied, or for the ecstatic creativity those longings once evoked, there would be no church there at all. And one knows this, however fleetingly, in the instant of their apparition.

After all—and this is a truth so certain that only the most doctrinaire Marxist or lumpen British atheist could deny it—the structure of culture is essentially an idealist one, and a living culture is a spiritual dispensation. A civilization's values, symbols, ideals, and imaginative capacities flow down from above, from the most exalted objects of its transcendental desires, and a people's greatest collective achievements are always in some sense attempts to translate eternal into temporal order. This will always be especially obvious in places of worship. To wax vaguely Heideggerean, temples are built to summon the gods, but only because the gods have first called out to mortals. There are invisible powers (whether truly divine powers or only powers of the imagination) that seek to become manifest, to emerge from their invisibility, and they can do this only by inspiring human beings to wrest beautiful forms out of intractable elements. They disclose their unseen world by transforming this world into its concrete image, allegory, or reflection, in a few privileged places where divine and human gazes briefly meet.

Such places, moreover, are only the most concentrated crystallizations of a culture's highest visions of the good, true, and beautiful; they are not isolated retreats, set apart from the society around them, but are rather the most intense expressions of that society's rational and poetic capacities. And it is under the shelter of the heavens made visible in such places that all of a people's laws and institutions, admirable or defective, take shape, as well as all its arts, civic or private, sacred or profane, festal or ordinary. This is a claim not about private beliefs, or about the particular motives that may have led to any particular law or work of art, but about the conceptual and aesthetic resources that any culture can possess or impart, and those are determined by religious traditions—by shared pictures of eternity, shared stories of the absolute. That is why the very concept of a secular civilization is nearly meaningless.

This is also to say, incidentally, that a culture's greatest source of strength is a source of considerable fragility as well. When the momentary thrill induced by the angels of Sacré-Cœur subsides, what remains is merely a certain poignancy: the realization that the emotional power of those figures, insofar as it cannot be accounted for merely by a trick of the light, emanates entirely from the past. It has nothing to do with the future. Given the late date of the basilica's construction, and given the realities of modern France, it is impossible not to see that splendidly overwhelming but very temporary act of disclosure as a valedictory performance, a last epiphany before a final departure, at the end of a cultural history that now shows no capacity for renewing itself. Civilization is a spiritual labor, an openness to revelation, a venture of faith, subsisting to a great degree on things no more substantial than myths and visions and prophetic dreams; thus it can be destroyed not only by invading armies or economic collapse, but also by simple disenchantment.

All of which brings me to my topic: the uncertainties of the American future and the possible role religion may or may not play in that future. If it seems I have taken a rather roundabout approach to the issue, my earnest defense is that, to this point, I have been talking all along about America; I have simply been doing so *sub contrario*. American religious life, in all its native expressions, is so odd and paradoxical that it is often most easily approached indirectly, stealthily, from behind, as it were; and, to my mind, one of the best ways of doing this is to begin one's approach from France. The contrast is so edifyingly stark. So much of what historically made France a great nation is all but entirely absent from America, while so much of what has made America a great nation is all but entirely alien to France, and it may be the case that many of the principal weaknesses of each are among the other's principal strengths.

This is not, of course, a comparison between two distinct civilizations—at least, not if one uses that word in its grandest, most inflexible, and haughtiest sense. America's chief originality lies in the political, social, and economic experiment that it undertook at its founding, but it is a very young nation, and delightfully diverse, and its culture is largely a blended distillation of other cultures. Often blamelessly derivative, but also often shamefully forgetful of even the recent past, it is a nation that floats lightly upon the depths of human history, with sometimes too pronounced a sense of its own novelty.

So, obviously, there is no American equivalent of Sacré-Cœur: some consecrated space haunted by the glories and failures of a deep past, ennobled and burdened by antique hopes and fantasies, emblematic of an ancient people's whole spiritual story, but also eloquent of spiritual disappointment and the waning of faith. There are places of local memory, especially in the South, but their scope is rather severely circumscribed. America's churches, when they are not merely serviceable clapboard meetinghouses or tents of steel and glass, are mostly just imitations of European originals: imported, transplanted, always somewhat out of place. They tell us practically nothing about America itself, and even less about whatever numinous presences might be hovering overhead.

Yet those presences are there. There may not be a distinctive American civilization in the fullest sense, but there definitely is a distinctly American Christianity. It is something protean, scattered, fragmentary, and fissile, often either mildly or exorbitantly heretical, and sometimes only vestigially Christian, but it can nevertheless justly be called the American religion—and it is a powerful religion. It is, however, a style of faith remarkably lacking in beautiful material forms or coherent institutional structures, not by accident, but essentially. Its civic inexpressiveness is a consequence not simply of cultural privation, or of frontier simplicity, or of modern utilitarianism, or even of some lingering Puritan reserve towards ecclesial rank and architectural ostentation, but also of a profound and radical resistance to outward forms. It is a religion of the book or of private revelation, of oracular wisdom and foolish rapture, but not one of tradition, hierarchy, or public creeds. Even where it creates intricate institutions of its own, and erects its own large temples, it tends to do so entirely on its own terms: in a void, in a cultural and (ideally) physical desert, at a fantastic remove from all traditional sources of authority, historical "validity," or good taste (Mormonism is an expression of this tendency at its boldest, most original, and most effervescently vulgar). What America shares with, say, France is the general Western heritage of Christian belief, with all its confessional variations; what it has never had any real part in, however, is Christendom.

In one sense, this is not at all surprising. America was born in flight from the Old World's thrones and altars, the corrupt accommodations between spiritual authority and earthly power, the old confusion of reverence for God with servility before princes. And, as a political project in its own right, the United States was the first Western nation explicitly founded upon principles requiring no official alliance between religious confession and secular government. Even if this had not been so, the ever-greater religious heterogeneity of America over the course of its history would surely, sooner or later, have made such an alliance absurdly impractical. And so, in fact, America was established as the first truly modern nation, the first Western society consciously to dissociate its constitutional order from the political mythologies of a long disintegrating Christendom, and the first predominantly Christian country to place itself under, at most, God's general providential supervision, but not under the command of any of his officially recognized lieutenants. The nation began, one could argue, from a place at which the other nations of the West had not yet arrived.

In another sense, however, when one considers the result, it is all rather astonishing. America may have arisen out of the end of Christendom, and as the first fully constituted political alternative to Christendom, but it somehow avoided the religious and cultural fate of the rest of the modern West. Far from blazing a trail into the post-Christian future that awaited other nations, America went quite a different way, down paths that no other Western society would ever tread, or even know how to find. Whereas European society—moving with varying speed but in a fairly uniform direction—experienced the end of Christendom simultaneously as the decline of faith, in America just the opposite happened. Here, the paucity of institutional and "civilizing" mediations between the transcendent and the immanent went hand in hand with a general, largely formless, and yet utterly irrepressible intensification of faith: rather than the exhaustion of religious longing, its revival; rather than a long nocturnal descent into disenchantment, a new dawning of early Christianity's elated expectation of the Kingdom.

I should, I suppose, avoid excessive generalization on this matter. Just about every living religion has found some kind of home here, bringing along whatever institutional supports it could fit into its luggage. Many such creeds have even managed to preserve the better part of their integrity. Still, I would argue (maybe with a little temerity), such communities exist here as displaced fragments of other spiritual worlds, embassies from more homogeneous religious cultures, and it is from those cultures that they derive whatever cogency they possess. They are beneficiaries of the hospitable and capacious indeterminacy of American spirituality, but not direct expressions of it. The form of Christianity most truly *indigenous* to America is one that is simultaneously peculiarly disembodied and indomitably vigorous, and its unity is one of temperament rather than confession. The angels of America have remained, for the most part, unseen presences, unable or unwilling to emerge from their hiddenness into the open visibility of a shared material or intellectual culture; and yet, perhaps for this very reason, they have also retained the sort of terrible force that their Old World counterparts lost some time ago.

They may, therefore, be very clever angels. Never coming out of the shadows in great national churches, or dancing attendance on kings, or lending much of a hand in civil government, they also never risked being weighed down by human political history. Because they never revealed themselves too carelessly to the eyes of faith, they also never exposed themselves to the scornful gaze of disbelief. France's angels, by contrast, had for centuries been perceived as complicit in the injustices of the *ancien régime,* and so could hardly claim immunity when the old order fell, or escape the resentments and skepticisms that that order had bred. But America's angels have kept their mysterious transcendence intact to this day, and with it their power to inspire spiritual longings, even of the most extravagant kind.

None of this is to say, however, that American society has somehow really succeeded in erecting a partition between its religious and its civic identities. Cult and culture are never separable, even if their relation does not involve any explicit union between a particular religious body and the power of the state. American spirituality may be particularly rich in those kinds of devotion that are most elusive of stable institutional form: enthusiasm and ecstasy, apocalyptic mysticism and gnostic individualism, dreams and visions. But, even so, America is—as much as any nation has ever been—its religion, and its greatest cultural virtues and defects are all bound up with the kinds of faith that flourish here.

Years ago, as an aid to teaching undergraduates and a partial remedy to the boredom of the lecture hall, I devised a needlessly florid typology for describing the various shapes taken by modern Western nations in Christendom's aftermath and the various ways in which Western societies have gathered up the fragments of the old concords between church and state. As a mnemonic device for my students, it was a ghastly failure, but, as a useful oversimplification, it was a spectacular triumph (which makes it baffling that, with the exception of a partial reference to it in an article in *The New Criterion* some years back, I have never thought to put it in print until now). I told my students to think of modern Western nations, and of their diverse attitudes towards the social and political remains of the old Christian order, under three figures—pseudomorphs, exuviae, and poltergeists—and I proposed, as an example of each type respectively, the Soviet Union, France, and the United States.

Pseudomorphism—for those who have not recently leafed through manuals of crystallography or volumes of Spengler—is that process by which one crystal assumes the alien shape of another, through chemical or molecular substitution, or by being forced into the space evacuated by its predecessor. It seemed to me an elegant metaphor for the way that, for instance, Soviet political culture had supplanted the late Russian version of Byzantine Caesaropapism not just by dissolving the latter's basic forms, but by trying to colonize them from within: in place of the old authoritarianism, a new absolutism, with a more comprehensive state apparatus and a more fanatical intolerance of heresy; in place of Eastern Orthodoxy's emphasis upon eternity within time and the light of the Kingdom amid history's darkness, the Soviet faith in the providential sovereignty of material dialectic and the ineluctability of the socialist utopia; in place of the ethereal gold and temperas of Byzantine iconography, the shrill vermilion and lifeless opacity of Soviet realist portraiture; in place of the relics of incorruptible saints, Lenin's pickled cadaver in a glass box; and so on.

Exuviation, on the other hand, is the shedding of skins or shells, and exuviae are what are sloughed off. The image works especially well if one thinks of those translucent integumental husks that cicadas leave behind them, clinging tenaciously to the bark of trees. It is an apt metaphor for all those enchanting vestiges of religious tradition found in societies that, like France, have lost the faith so thoroughly that even the passion of revolutionary impiety has long since subsided. There the remains of the old order are reduced to ornamental souvenirs, the lovely traces of vanished dream-worlds; they just linger on, quietly, in old buildings, museums, tastes, customs, the calendar, turns of phrase, shared stories, a few legal traditions, a few moral premises, a few imperturbable pillars of cultural sensibility, but everything that once inhabited, shaped, and animated them is gone. They are exquisitely dead. They can excite indifference, tender memories, casual contempt, but rarely love or belief. They have become elements of a general aesthetic and moral atmosphere, and nothing more.

As for poltergeists, there the image is less obscure. Everything I have already said about American religion explains the metaphor: a force capable of moving material realities about, often unpredictably and even alarmingly, and yet possessing no proper, stable material form of its own. American religion lacks the imposing structures of culture, law, and public worship that Christendom evolved over the centuries, but its energy is almost impossible to contain. It has no particular social place, and yet it is everywhere.

If this typology, however, seems a little too dainty or a little too neat, it might be better simply to talk in terms of the relative vitality of (excuse the postmodern fillip here) "force and structure" in a nation's religion. Soviet society, by grotesquely inverting rather than destroying the religious grammar of Russian culture, showed that both the spiritual and the institutional aspects of Russian Christendom, however diminished at the time of the revolution, still had a little life in them. The serene urbanity of today's French secularism, the pragmatic laicism of French republicanism, and the relaxed anticlericalism of French society as a whole testify to French Christendom's absolute dormancy in all its aspects. In the case of either nation, though, religious force and structure persisted or declined more or less together. In America, by contrast, as happened nowhere else, they suffered a schism, fairly early on, whose result—or, at any rate, sequel—was that religion's public structure was shattered, but the force contained within it was released.

One might have expected that a spirituality without the tangible support of civic religion would disperse over time, but perhaps the passion of faith often thrives best when it is largely unaccommodated, roaming on its own in wild places. After all, when one considers the first three centuries of Christian history, when the faith had no such support, it may make perfect sense that, in the wake of Christendom's collapse, the forms of Christianity that would prove most lively would be those that possess something analogous to the apocalyptic consciousness of the earliest Christian communities: their sense of having emerged from history into the immediacy of a unique redemptive event; their triumphant contempt for antique cult and culture; their experience of emancipation from the bondage of the law; their aloofness from structures of civil power; and their indifference to the historical future (for the present things are passing away).

There may even be some advantage in the absence of strong institutional organization, at least in certain circumstances. It may well be that the translation of Christianity's original apocalyptic ferment into a cultural logic and social order produced a powerful but necessarily volatile alloy. For all the good that this transformation produced in the shaping of Western civilization (which no sane person could deny), it also encumbered the faith with a weight of historical and cultural expectation wholly incompatible with the gospel it proclaimed. Certainly Christian culture has excelled, as no other ever has, at incubating militant atheisms and even self-conscious nihilisms, and this may have something to do with its own innate tension between spiritual rebellion and social piety. Perhaps the concrescence of Christianity into Christendom necessarily led in Europe, over the course of centuries, to its gradual mortification, its slow attrition through internal stress, and finally its dissipation into the inconclusiveness of human history and the ephemerality of political orders. The relation between force and structure had become so hardened by the end that the one could not escape the fate of the other.

Whatever the case, the American religion somehow slipped free from this story before it reached its dénouement, and so it is not inextricably entangled in the tragic contradictions of historical memory. At its purest, in fact, it is free of almost all memory, and so of all anxiety: it strives towards a state of almost perfect timelessness, seeking a place set apart from the currents of human affairs, where God and the soul can meet and, so to speak, affirm one another. For a faith so thoroughly divorced from history, there is no set limit to the future it may possess. And if, as I have said, culture is always shaped by spiritual aspirations, this all has a very great bearing on what kind of future America might possess. History is not created by historical consciousness, after all; the greatest historical movements are typically inspired by visions of an eternal truth that has somehow overtaken history. This is simply because a people's very capacity for a future, at least one of any duration or consequence (good or bad), requires a certain obliviousness in regard to time's death-bound banality, a certain imaginative levity, a certain faith. The future is often the gift of the eternal.

I have gone some distance, I suppose, without offering some specific example of this "American religion" I keep referring to. This is because I really do understand it as something intrinsically impalpable and shapeless: a diffuse and pervasive spiritual temper rather than a particular creed. But, for clarity's sake, I may as well admit that I regard American Evangelicalism in all its varieties—fundamentalist, Pentecostal, blandly therapeutic—as the most pristine expression of this temper. I say this not because of Evangelicalism's remarkable demographic range, its dominance in certain large regions of the country, or its extraordinary missionary success in Latin America and elsewhere, but simply because I am convinced of its autochthony: it is a form of spiritual life that no other nation could have produced, and the one most perfectly in accord with the special genius and idiocy, virtue and vice, of American culture.

Whatever one's view of Evangelicalism, only bigotry could prevent one from recognizing its many admirable features: the dignity, decency, and probity it inspires in individuals, families, and communities; the moral seriousness it nourishes in countless consciences; its frequent and generous commitment to alleviating the sufferings of the indigent and ill; its capacity for binding diverse peoples together in a shared spiritual resolve; its power to alter character profoundly for the better; the joy it confers. But, conversely, only a deep ignorance of Christian history could blind one to its equally numerous eccentricities: the odd individualism of its understanding of salvation; its bizarre talk of Christ as one's "personal Lord and savior"; its fantastic scriptural literalism; the crass sentimentality of some of its more popular forms of worship; its occasional tendency to confuse piety with patriotism.

I am frequently tempted to describe it as a kind of "Christian Bhakti," a pure ecstatic devotionalism, as opposed to those more "Vedic" forms of Christianity that ground themselves in ancient traditions. Much of American Evangelicalism not only lacks any sense of tradition, but is blithely hostile to tradition on principle: What is tradition, after all, other than man-made history, and what is history other than exile from paradise? What need does one have of tradition when one has the Bible, that eternal love letter from Jesus to the soul, inerrant, unambiguous, uncorrupted by the vicissitudes of human affairs? In some of its most extreme forms, Evangelicalism is a religion of total and unsullied reverie, the pure present of the child's world, where ingenuous outcries and happy gestures and urgent conjurations instantly bring forth succor and substance. And, at its most intensely fundamentalist, so precipitous is its flight from the gravity of history into Edenic and eschatological rapture that it reduces all of cosmic history to a few thousand years of terrestrial existence and the whole of the present to a collection of signs urgently pointing to the world's imminent ending.

Now, I know I am describing only a few extreme variants of only one variant of Protestant Christianity in America. I might point out that I am also, however, describing acute forms of a spirituality whose chronic forms can be found liberally distributed throughout America's religious communities, even in certain circles within American Catholicism, Judaism, mainstream Protestantism, and elsewhere. That, though, is of only passing interest. My central claim is that what one sees with particular clarity in Evangelical piety is a deep spiritual orientation that both informs and expresses the American mythos: that grand narrative, going back to colonial times, of a people that has fled the evils of an Old World sunk in corruption, cast off the burden of an intolerable past, and been "born again" as a new nation, redeemed from the violence and falsehood of the former things.

It is not difficult, of course, to enumerate the weaknesses of a culture shaped by such a spiritual logic. It is a spirituality that, for example, makes very little contribution to the aesthetic surface of American life. This is no small matter. The American religion does almost nothing to create a shared high culture, to enrich the lives of ordinary persons with the loveliness of sacred public spaces, to erect a few durable bulwarks against the cretinous barbarity of late modern popular culture, or to enliven the physical order with intimations of transcendent beauty. With its nearly absolute separation between inward conviction and outward form, it is largely content to surrender the surrounding world to utilitarian austerity. It could not do otherwise, even if the nation's constitution were not formally so secular. It would not have the imaginative resources. It is a religion of feeling, not of sensibility; it might be able to express itself in great scale, but not as a rule in good taste.

It is, however, a religious temperament wonderfully free of cynicism or moral doubt, and so it may have a singular capacity for surviving historical disappointment and the fluctuations of national fortune. Its immunity to disenchantment seems very real, at any rate. It may, in fact, grow only stronger if the coming decades should bring about a decline in America's preeminence, power, international influence, or even solvency. Whatever the case, it is unlikely to lapse very easily into a decline of its own, or vanish into some American equivalent of the spiritual exhaustion and moral lassitude of post-Christian Europe.

For myself, I should confess that I approach the relation between America's cultural and religious futures with an insoluble ambivalence. This is, in part, because I have no emotional investment in America's pre-eminence among modern powers. Our geopolitical ascendancy during the latter half of the twentieth century was very much an accident, and not a very pleasant one. It was the result of the country being dragged back into a history of which it had taken leave centuries before, and into the psychotic savagery of mid-century European affairs, and into a global ideological struggle for the future.

It would not be any great tragedy if all of that should now prove to have been a very transient episode. In relative terms, American prosperity and power will remain formidable enough for some time, and I cannot see why anyone should fret over anything as intrinsically worthless as global "leadership." The question that should concern us, it seems to me, is whether in years ahead America will produce a society that has any particular right to a future. By this, I mean nothing more elaborate than: How charitable and just a society will it be, how conscious will it be of those truths that transcend the drearier economies of finite existence, and will it produce much good art? And all of that will be determined, inevitably, by spiritual forces

It is not obvious, however, what those forces will be, or what they will bring about. It is very much an open and troubling question whether American religiosity has the resources to help sustain a culture *as* a culture— whether, that is, it can create a meaningful future, or whether it can only prepare for the end times. Is the American religious temperament so apocalyptic as to be incapable of culture in any but the most local and ephemeral sense? Does it know of any city other than Babylon the Great or the New Jerusalem? For all the moral will it engenders in persons and communities, can it cultivate the kind of moral intelligence necessary to live in eternity and in historical time simultaneously, without contradiction? Will its lack of any coherent institutional structure ultimately condemn it to haunting rather than vivifying its culture, or make it too susceptible to exploitation by alien interests, or render it incapable of bearing any sufficiently plausible or even interesting witness to the transcendent...? And so on and so on. There is much to admire in the indigenous American religious sensibility, without question, but also much to deplore, and there is plenteous cause for doubt here.

Still, the worst fate that could befall America, one far grimmer than the mere loss of some of its fiscal or political supremacy in the world, would be the final triumph of a true cultural secularism. I know that there are those on both the left and the right who still believe in the project of an "enlightened" secular society; some—curiously ignorant of pre-modern and modern history alike—actually cling to the delusion that secular society on the whole is a kinder, fairer, and freer arrangement than any known to earlier ages. And, then again, one does not need to be quite that credulous to be profoundly grateful (as I am, for instance) for the dissolution of the old alliance between religious orthodoxies and the mechanisms of political power. Nevertheless, whatever one may say in favor of secularism's more agreeable political expressions, its record to this point, as an ideology or a material history, has been mixed at best: monstrous warfare, totalitarian regimes, genocides, the inexorable expansion of the power and province of the state, the gradual decline of the arts and of civic aesthetics. . . . It can scarcely be taken very seriously as the model of what a society ideally ought to be.

Even when it is not breeding great projects for the rectification of human nature or human society—not building death-camps or gulags, not preaching eugenics or the workers' paradise—the secularist impulse can create nothing of enduring value. It corrupts the will and the imagination with the deadening boredom of an ultimate pointlessness, weakens the hunger for the good, true, and beautiful, makes the pursuit of diversion life's most pressing need, and gives death the final word. A secular people—by which I mean not simply a people with a secular constitution, but one that really no longer believes in any reality beyond the physical realm—is a dying people, both culturally and demographically. Civilization, or even posterity, is no longer worth the effort. And, in our case, it would not even be a particularly dignified death. European Christendom has at least left a singularly presentable corpse behind. If the American religion were to evaporate tomorrow, it would leave behind little more than the brutal banality of late modernity.

In the end, though, on the matter of religion and the American future, I am certain of very little. I know only how unprecedented and hence unpredictable our historical situation is. The angels of Sacré-Cœur are now, for the most part, sublime symbols of an absence; once images of a seemingly inexhaustible supernatural source of cultural possibility, they have become little more than ironic evocations of a final cultural impotence. They were raised aloft in the fading twilight of a long, magnificent, and terrible epoch, during which a glorious vision of eternal splendor was given profuse and enduring concrete form, but they were not the harbingers of a cultural renewal. America, by contrast, has never known either that glory or that failure. Our angels continue to move in their inaccessible heavens, apparently still calling out to mortals, still able to provoke our sons and daughters to prophesy, our old men to dream dreams, our young men to see visions. So who knows? Perhaps the quieter strengths they impart to our culture—its deeper reserves of charity and moral community, the earnestness of its spiritual longings, its occasional poetic madness—will persist for a long while yet, and with them the possibility of cultural accomplishments far more important than mere geopolitical preeminence. There is, at any rate, some room for hope.

Everybody Gets Rich

Kevin D. Williamson

I HAVE BEEN ENGAGED in a little high-low reading in the past several months, alternating one highbrow work (e.g., *Outer Dark*) with one less exalted work (e.g. *Lonesome Dove*). My most recent pairing was the short stories of Raymond Carver, which I had not read, and Stephen King's *The Stand*, which I had read as a youngster and wanted to revisit to see whether it retained any of the fascination it had on first encounter. There is a great deal going on in these works, though a great deal less going on in Mr. Carver's stories than in Mr. King's. In Mr. Carver's, people in various stages of marital disintegration get drunk and behave badly. In Mr. King's novel, well ... there's a secret underground government lab incubating a superplague, and a guy who's just hit it big as a pop star, who goes home to visit his mother in the Bronx, and a General Ripper–type plotting against the Russkies, and so on. But they're the same story, really: the story of the world ending. In Mr. Carver's short stories, the world ends one unhappy family at a time, in *The Stand* the whole world takes it in the neck at once.

The thing that struck me most strongly in both works, though, wasn't the spectacular horrors—the ravages of alcoholism, adultery, wife-beating, doomsday viruses—

but the quotidian horror of economic insecurity. Mr. King was writing *The Stand* at the same time Mr. Carver was discovering Alcoholics Anonymous and beginning his second life, and each offers a testament to one undeniable fact about life in the late 1970s: People were poor. Americans were the richest people in the world even after Jimmy Carter got through with them, and globalization hadn't extended to the point at which the American middle class was competing head-to-head with poor Asians, Latin Americans, and Eastern Europeans. But, damn, people were poor, at least from the point of view of 2011. There's a bit in *The Stand* when the newly hatched pop star notices that his mother has gone the full fatted calf for her prodigal son, buying, among other things, two pounds of butter. He wonders how his mother, who is of quite modest means but gainfully employed and self-sufficient, was able to afford such an extravagance as two pounds of butter. Who worries about the price of butter today? A pound of butter runs, typically, about $2.50, but a careful shopper can buy a pound of butter for less than $1. Very fancy butter from Whole Foods runs less than $4 a pound. Anybody too poor to buy a pound of butter in 2011 will have a pound of butter bought for him, no questions asked.

There's a whole economics in the price of a pound of butter: Adjusted for inflation, a pound of butter cost nearly $7 a hundred years ago, about three times what it costs today. By the time of *The Stand*, it was down to about $6 a pound in inflation-adjusted dollars. And it has fallen further faster. But not everywhere: In Norway, as of this writing, a combination of protectionist trade policies and bad luck has sent the cost of butter to nearly $500/pound—prosperity only emerges when governments allow it to emerge. In 1950, the typical family had to dedicate more than one-third of household income to buying groceries. Today, that number runs from 10 percent to 14 percent, and a great many households spend more eating out than they do on groceries.

I noticed a fellow at the recent Occupy Wall Street protests carrying a sign reading: "They eat filet mignon. I eat the dollar menu." This of course says a great deal, and not at all what he meant for it to say. Here is an American man in apparently good health complaining that, while he can have a modest meal for 8 minutes and 30 seconds of work at the minimum wage in New York, (including the sales tax)—and have somebody else cook it for him, at that—he'd really rather have filet mignon, thanks very much.

I sympathize: Earning the New York minimum wage, he could report for work at 9 A.M. and by noon have earned enough to have a two-inch thick USDA prime twenty-one-day-aged filet mignon for lunch, providing he is willing to cook it himself. If he reports back to work at 1 P.M., he must then work until 3:15 P.M. to pay the rent on his modest New York City apartment ($500/month in the Bronx, via Craigslist, with hardwood floors, heat, and hot water included) and then until about 3:45 P.M. to pay for his monthly subway pass or to make the lease payment on his Kia—which, at $99 a month, is a bit less expensive than the subway pass, but then there's gasoline and insurance to think about. The money he earns between then and 6 P.M. ought to be sufficient to cover his other meals and incidentals, if he's thrifty, though he'll probably need to put in a few extra shifts a month or get some overtime to keep current on his taxes.

Filet mignon every day, a private car, an apartment of his own—Mr. Minimum Wage is not only living better than most of the people currently living and 99 percent of the people who ever have lived, he's also living substantially better than a typical American middle manager did a generation ago, to say nothing of a workingman. He must make decisions and prioritize his expenses, but his tradeoffs are between having an automobile of his own or taking the subway and having a cell phone.

It is worth taking an economic eye to one's literature. My own childhood hero, the Count of Monte Cristo, dazzles his guests by serving fish from two distant parts of the world—a millionaire's whim, he calls it. Alexandre Dumas simply could not have imagined a Wal-Mart big box store, which, on average, is 185,000 square feet of retail space, offering well more than 200,000 products gathered from around the world for shoppers who enjoy, without even thinking about it, riches that the Count could not have imagined: air conditioning while they shop, refrigeration to keep their food fresh, etc. Which is to say, we are not a nation of paupers. From energy used to calories consumed to travel enjoyed to the size of our houses to the variety of our diets and distractions, we are rich, rich, rich, besotted with wealth, drowning in affluence, up to our fat little earlobes in the good life. So why do we feel so poor?

Not everything has followed the economics of butter—getting more plentiful, better, and cheaper every year. Some things have out-buttered butter, of course: Our gadgets, our cell phones, much of our food, and even many of our vacations were available only to the very rich a few decades ago, if they were available at all. It is hard to imagine, watching the general public come and go through the security theater at an American airport, that air travel once was so rarified and glamorous as to produce that brilliantly evocative midcentury noun: the jet set. But some important things have not managed to keep up with the brilliant technological and economic innovation of a sophisticated product such as butter. Perhaps the most important one of those things is Leviathan, whose buttery, blubbery bulk keeps getting more expensive and less effective.

The welfare state isn't a very good buy. The average Social Security benefit runs just over $1,100 a month—peanuts, hardly enough to keep you in cut-rate butter once your median rent of more than $800 has been paid. For that, you're taxed 12 percent of your take-home pay. Compare that to this: A married couple, each earning the minimum wage, investing only 10 percent of their earnings at a modest 7 percent return, retires with an annual income of more than $100,000 a year—even if they never touch the $1.5 million principle they'll leave to their children. President George W. Bush was mocked for calling his proposal to cultivate such minimum-wage millionaires the "Ownership Society," but it was the most important initiative of his presidency. Yes, I have included the War on Terror in that estimate. Conservatives who faithfully supported President Bush's grandiose, heart-of-gold/brain-of-cabbage program to make Anglo-Saxon republicans out of obscure desert savages left him naked and friendless in the entitlement-reform fight. But reality is not optional: Just as the ghost of George W. Bush haunts President Barack Obama's national-defense policy—which now incorporates such concessions to reality as open-ended Gitmo sequestrations and rendition, "enhanced" interrogations, pre-emptive warfare, and even the premeditated assassination of American citizens (something Dick Cheney never had the brass to propose, in public at least)—so does the specter of the Ownership Society lurk in the dark corners of our current fiscal crisis. Happily, it is a friendly ghost.

Winston Churchill famously observed that Americans can always be counted on to do the right thing—after exhausting every other option. Our economic and fiscal options are diminishing daily. The U.S. Treasury has now had its Pearl Harbor—the downgrade—and, as with the war against Hirohito and his wild boys, this one involves fighting a lot of zeros: for instance, the fourteen ugly aughts needed to write out our real national debt, which includes $15 trillion or so in explicit federal debt, another $100 trillion in entitlement liabilities disappeared like so many Latin American dissidents through the miracle of government accounting, several trillion in unfunded pension and health-care liabilities for government employees, trillions more in state and local debt, and several relatively trivial trillions sprinkled hither and yon. *Annus domini* 2012, it adds up to $130 trillion to $140 trillion. That figure is, literally, more than all the money in the world—more than every piece of currency in any denomination issued by any government, along with all of the money in the world's checking and savings accounts, certificates of deposit, money-market funds, and other forms of ready money. About twice that, in fact. It is more than twice the annual economic output of human civilization. All of which is to say, it's not the sort of fiscal imbalance that is going to get solved by raising taxes on Wall Street sharks or eliminating foreign-aid payments.

And this is a very excellent thing. At the risk of taking a Shining Path approach to reform, fiscal realists ought to welcome the pending crisis in American public finances with almost as much glee as dread: This is how we all get rich! Leviathan is over—*so* 20th century! Americans are not, in the majority, stupid. They do not wish to be paupers—and they aren't. Three-tenths of the population is functionally illiterate, and one-tenth is so highly educated that it is capable of entertaining the most preposterous notions (check out the shelves at a New Age bookstore or revisit some of Barack Obama's campaign materials if you doubt this), but that leaves a solid 60 percent of the people of the most prosperous and powerful nation in the history of human civilization who do not want to be poor, miserable, and vulnerable, and who have the power to reshape our ailing institutions to ensure that they are not left so. In this effort, they will get some help from unlikely quarters, including from the Chinese police state, whose masters also do not wish to see Americans impoverished and immiserated, if only for their own narrow, selfish purposes. (And who can blame them? A serious depression in the United States would send unemployment skyrocketing in China, and Chinese economic crises do not end with elections, but with massacres.)

As the U.S. Treasury runs out of money to lavish upon cowboy-poet festivals, cocaine binges for monkeys, transgressive/transsexual/transformative/dykes-against-the-gender-binary performance art evenings in Omaha, superhighways connecting nowhere with nowhere, and the like, Americans will, perforce, begin to engage in a salubrious debate about what government actually should be doing—and what it is good at doing. In terms of stuff that you really want the national state in charge of, the U.S. Marine Corps will no doubt continue to look pretty solid, and dubious grants to community-organizing rackets will not.

That debate will not be held at the federal level only. It is worth noting that total government spending in the United States is about the same as in Canada, once the states and localities are added to the mix. We do not have small government in the United States—we have dispersed and dysfunctional government. A textbook example of that phenomenon recently made headlines when the town fathers of Topeka, Kansas, voted to legalize wife-beating. Seriously: Topeka repealed its domestic-violence statute. The city of Topeka was in a pissing contest with Shawnee County, which surrounds it, over who would bear the expense of prosecuting domestic-violence cases. Shawnee County's authorities said they no longer could afford to do so, and told Topeka it would have to prosecute the cases itself. Topeka therefore repealed its domestic-violence law, leaving the county as the only prosecutor with jurisdiction over the crime. Naturally, shock and outrage followed, with women's advocates raising a ruckus that was, for once, well merited. They pointed to a woman who had been beaten with a crowbar and thrown through a plate-glass window by her beau. Under Kansas law, that is misdemeanor domestic violence, and budget cuts meant that misdemeanor cases are not being prosecuted. (Nobody, save your obedient servant, got around to asking: Why is beating a woman with a crowbar and throwing her through a plate-glass window a *misdemeanor*, rather than a *felony?*)

"This is what austerity looks like," the liberal MSNBC host Chris Hayes said of the sorry situation. But of course that poor woman's bloodied visage and her lack of recourse to the law is not the face of austerity: It is the face of government's inability to make elementary rational decisions about the allocation of scarce resources—and resources always are by definition scarce, recession or no. Excluding its public schools, Topeka, a city of about 120,000, spends $222 million a year during these bleak days of austerity, maintains one full-time municipal employee for every ten residents, spends six-figure sums on arts funds, offers its city manager nearly $200,000 a year in compensation. The mayor's secretary costs more than $100,000 a year to employ, while the nine employees of the city manager's and city clerk's offices cost an average of nearly $100,000 a head. Presumably, there are some powerful municipal-employee unions at work here, which would explain why, at the time of this writing, the city was advertising for labor-relation specialists at $90,000 each. The nine employees of the city's HR department bring in an average of about $64,000 in salary. There's a six-figure fire chief and a fire *marshal,* too, overseeing a fire-prevention program that employs eight people at more than $100,000 a year on average. This is not what austerity looks like. This is what politics run amok looks like. And lest you think that Topeka is some sort of remarkably spendthrift municipal outlier, note this: The city was given a budgeting award by the nationwide Government Finance Officers Association in 2010.

Until the year before last, Topeka also maintained a five-member citywide sensitivity department ("human relations") that was running through $300,000 a year in salaries and another fifty grand in contracted services. That has been reduced to zero employees at $0.00 per annum. Politicians do not learn quickly, but they do learn. Today it's the P.C. police in Topeka vs. the fire department. Tomorrow, it's a choice between the Pacific Fleet and Social Security. In truth, anchoring the Pacific Fleet would cover only a tiny bit of Social Security. Cutting Department of Defense spending to $0.00 would not cover Social Security. And, as spelled out above, we have really good alternatives to Social Security. We do not, at present, have an alternative to the Pacific Fleet. Advantage: squids.

It will be considerably easier to create a market-based alternative to Social Security when there are no more Social Security checks being cut—and they are *not* going to be cut (cf. that $100 trillion unfunded liability). If we're lucky and smart, we'll start doing it before the Social Security checks stop. And it won't just be Social Security: Medicare and Medicaid are going away, too, whether we like it or not. Most of the welfare state will either wither away entirely or be severely truncated. Americans will have the opportunity to rediscover such hoary-sounding virtues as thrift and independence, and their joint product, liberty. All of which turns out to be worth having in a way that is not nearly so corny and Tea Party–sounding and tricorn-wearing as you might think. That's the optimistic take, and there is reason to believe that this is the more accurate forecast.

There are, broadly speaking, three ways in which the public finances of the United States of America might be rationalized. One is through the democratic political process. (Stop laughing.) (No, really, stop laughing.) It is not unimaginable that, with the body politic finally fired up about the head-clutching scale of the debt, some sort of necessarily flawed and dirty but credible and achievable grand fiscal bargain will be struck. Most likely, that will come from combining something rather like the Simpson-Bowles deficit commission's tax plan—which achieves a net tax increase by reducing tax rates while eliminating all or most exclusions, as Jon Huntsman proposed during his Republican primary campaign—and the Ryan Roadmap entitlement-reform plan, which uses a number of market-based measures and old-fashioned spending cuts to reduce the Medicare/Medicaid footprint. Ryan's plan leaves Social Security untouched for now, and its reform can be put off for a while, but, ultimately, we're upside-down on the demographics, and the dwindling number of workers whose wages are being sequestered to support a booming number of retirees eventually will revolt.

While the ideal outcome would be to leave investment and retirement savings an entirely private matter, the more likely outcome is that workers will be obliged under law to invest approximately what they paid in Social Security taxes into one of several government-approved retirement funds. This will not be the worst thing that ever has happened to Americans, though it will remain gallingly paternalistic.

If the political class does not step up—and I doubt that it will—then the crisis in American public finances will be resolved through the marketplace. There are two ways for that to happen: slow and steady or fast and panicky. If it goes slow and steady, chances are excellent that we will come through our future monetary-fiscal crisis stronger and freer than we entered it. The latter possibility is more of a run-to-the-hills scenario. Assuming that Washington is either (the populist view) too lazy and stupid or (the scholarly view) too paralyzed by incompatible political incentives to forestall the crisis on its own, then our most reasonable option is to work to ensure that the ultimate resolution in the marketplace is a gradual and orderly one, not an overnight panic.

In all probability, markets will first begin to address the non-sustainability of American public finances through higher interest rates on U.S. sovereign debt. Interest rates did not rise on U.S. bonds and bills during the 2008–11 period, even after the downgrade from Standard & Poor's. Indeed, such savvy super-investors as Bill Gross of PIMCO, the world's largest bond fund, played it poorly. PIMCO dumped all of its U.S. debt and then issued a press release announcing the fact, a bit smugly, and promised to short the bond. In the event, demand for Treasuries remained strong, yields went down, and Mr. Gross found himself, in his own words, crying in his beer. Other doom-and-gloomers moderated their positions, but not by that much: Jim Rogers continued to point to the devaluation of the major currencies, a worldwide race to the bottom, and George Soros closed his hedge fund, returning the money to the investors. In each case, these investors expected the projection of endless federal deficits to manifest itself in the near term, either through higher interest rates or a declining dollar, possibly both. But investment forecasting is a very different business from watching the wheels of history turn and trying to discern which way Leviathan is skating. Investment managers have to get the timing just right, and here they didn't. But it is unlikely that interest rates will be able to stay at or near zero forever. As the United States continues to accumulate sovereign debt faster than its economy grows, interest rates will go up.

Rising interest rates will have some interesting consequences. The single truly non-negotiable item on the federal budget is interest payments on the national debt. Skip one of those and you can pretty much just turn out the lights. Think Argentina circa 2002. If we take Congressional Budget Office estimates of future federal debt at face value, a return to interest rates at historical long-term averages in the next few years would mean a rapid expansion of the cost of those interest payments, making them the No. 1 big-ticket item on the budget, overshadowing things like Social Security, Medicare, and defense spending. Interest payments alone would consume somewhere between one-third and one-half of all federal revenue—assuming federal revenue projections stayed on track. In reality, the recession that would surely ensue from the disruption caused by such an interest-rate spike would bite deeply into tax collections as business profits suffered and economic activity contracted.

Don't worry—it gets worse. There is no reason to believe that our historical long-term average of 6.5 percent or so is a ceiling on how high interest rates could go. When Ronald Reagan and Paul Volcker got serious about choking inflation to death in the early 1980s, interest rates broke the 20 percent mark. Again assuming more or less stable tax receipts—an unwarranted, optimistic assumption, which I use here only for purposes of illustration—you'd see interest payments of between 60 and 70 percent of federal revenues in that scenario. There is to my knowledge no good estimate of what such interest rates would actually do to the economy and to tax receipts, but it is not implausible that interest payments could in any given year approach 100 percent of federal revenue, or even exceed it. Our choice at that point would be either to default or to add new debt to pay for the interest on current debt, which would nearly guarantee an eventual default.

This risk is exacerbated by the fact that the U.S. government, enchanted by low current interest rates, has decided to rely more heavily upon short-term financing of its debt. The maturity schedule is not at an all-time low, but it is at the lower end of the range, meaning that we have a lot more cowboy-poet debt finances on short-term bills and notes than on thirty-year bonds. That makes the Treasury more vulnerable to sudden swings in debt-service expenses.

Those dire outcomes only hold true for a short and violent upswing in interest rates. In reality, bond investors will continue to compare the creditworthiness of the United States against other sovereign debtors and will probably continue to conclude, correctly, that the United States is a better bet than is Japan or the European Union, to say nothing of Russia, India, China, or any of the other also-rans. But they will continue to notice that the federal debt is growing more quickly than the economy and figure that into their calculations. We already are at the point where everybody can look at the chart and conclude that things are unsustainable. There is little or no question about that, absent some unforeseen economic miracle (such as an unexpected technological breakthrough) that is especially beneficial to the United States and produces a sustained period of growth at historically unusual rates, such as those of the Reagan boom or the dot-com boom.

Hoping for a boom is foolish: For one thing, many booms turn out to be bubbles (late-1990s tech shares, U.S. housing, European green-energy firms, etc.). It is the bubble, not the bust, that causes the malinvestment leading to recessions and economic suffering. The recessions are merely the periods during which the irrational arrangements entered into during the booms get sorted out. Even if a non-bubbly technological breakthrough were to appear on the economic horizon, it is unlikely that it would be something that the United States would be able to exploit to the exclusion or partial exclusion of national competitors. The state of our educational system, our household finances, and our capital markets, combined with the simple fact of globalization, mean that the profits reaped from such a breakthrough are as likely to turbocharge the economy of South Korea, India, or Singapore as that of the United States. The temptation to wait for a miracle and to put off hard choices with wishful thinking is probably the greatest economic threat we face.

It is worth noting that many of our long-term fiscal problems are the result of happy developments, not unhappy ones. Social Security is in trouble in part because of declining birth rates, but mostly because we live much, much longer than we did when the program was created.

In 1937, the first Social Security taxes were collected; in the decade leading up to that, more than 37,000 Americans died of malaria in the South alone. Not one of those poor Southerners went on to collect a Social Security check. (Today, nearly everybody who dies of malaria is a poor African—more on that in a second.) Our health-care spending is off the charts—both in government programs in the private sector (what is left of it)—because we do more

for more people, because we aren't killed off by pneumonia at sixty, and because we have higher expectations for our quality of life from cradle to grave. We are, in one sense, the national equivalent of the individual who never expected to live past sixty-five and didn't save adequately for his retirement. In the 1930s, it was hard to imagine that our average life expectancy for a white American woman would hit eighty-one years by the early twenty-first century. We're like Keith Richards: We never thought we'd live this long, and, while we do have the resources to take care of ourselves, we have to rethink some things. We can't keep appropriating like there's no tomorrow.

Likewise, the pressure on American middle-class wages from globalization, while painful to bear, is also a sign of the world's getting better: We Americans and Europeans are no longer the only rich and productive people in the world. Even those poor malaria-ridden Africans are getting in on the act. As the *Rational Optimist* author Matt Ridley put it in a recent *Times* of London op-ed:

The world economy as a whole has continued to grow: it shrank by just 0.6 percent in 2009 then rebounded upward by 5 percent in 2010, according to the IMF. The last four years have been rotten ones for us, but good ones for

Chinese, Indians, Brazilians, even Africans. Nigeria is growing at 9 percent a year.

Much of Africa, having stagnated in the 1980s and 1990s, has begun growing like an Asian tiger, incrementally raising life expectancy and living standards, inexorably cutting birthrates and poverty. Since Africa holds many of the world's poorest people, this is great news for anybody who cares about humanity as a whole. There is a long way to go, but the pessimists who said that Africa could never emulate Asia are increasingly being proved wrong.

Humanitarian sentiment compels us to celebrate the economic advancement of Asia and Africa. But it is not the only reason to celebrate their good fortune: We Americans make high-end stuff. It's hard to sell Boeing and Apple products to poor people.

While the private American economy faces some challenges, it also is presented with great opportunities by the emergence of a global middle class. It is American government initiatives, particularly in the social-welfare branches, that face deep and sometimes existential challenges. What that means is that minus the Big Boom or the Big Bust, we end up with the Big Bummer: a period during which the hard decisions that we have been putting off for a very long time—arguably, since the end of World War II—command our attention at last. The political fights will be acrimonious, but they will probably grow less so as possible options are rapidly foreclosed by economic realities. Our standard of living probably will continue to increase, but not so quickly as we had expected it to, and with a great deal more uncertainty and anxiety. At the risk of sounding cheaply rhetorical, anxiety and uncertainty are among the costs of liberty. Investors in the marketplace can win and they can lose, and none of the free-market solutions that emerge to supplant the welfare state will offer its greatest attraction: the absence of risk. Social Security, public schools, Medicaid—sure, they may stink, but they are guaranteed, and they can be relied upon, or so the story went.

Voters, like investors, do not have a bottomless appetite for risk, and while the entrepreneurially spirited and autistically libertarian may scoff, Americans from the Great Depression forward were collectively making a deliberate tradeoff between risk and return. They chose the lower-risk, lower-return model of the welfare state not because they were irrational, but because they were rational. The welfare state model catered to their preferences for the distribution of risk and reward better than the alternatives. Unfortunately, like the lords of finance and congressional barons who staked everything and more on the proposition that American houses are a magical commodity, the generations of Americans who acceded to the creation of the welfare state were working from a faulty set of economic assumptions. The welfare state does not, in the long run, reduce risk, any more than the securitization of mortgages reduced risk. It concentrates it, putting more and more economic decisions into the hands of political operators who have neither the information nor the incentives to make rational decisions. This, too, is a fact that is becoming increasingly clear in both the financial and political realms.

Unwinding the welfare state will not be easy or painless. Just as the sudden disappearance of several trillion dollars worth of home equity produced a nasty and extended recession, the disappearance of "equity" in future entitlement payments—a figure many times larger than the housing losses—will create a drag on economic growth. Never mind that these are only "paper" losses;

most of the housing losses were paper losses, too, since relatively few Americans were forced to sell their homes at a loss. Just as Americans had made plans for what to do with that $100,000 or $200,000 in home equity that they erroneously thought they had, Americans have made plans about how to spend their household finances—how to invest, how much to save, where to live, what kind of work to pursue, when and where to retire—based in part on faulty assumptions about future entitlement receipts. Put simply, there are a lot of Florida retirement condos that are never going to be bought by a lot of Wisconsin middle managers, a lot of cruises and vacations that are going to be skipped, a lot of grandkids' college funds that are not going to be topped up, and the like. In the aggregate, this will depress economic activity significantly, simply because people are going to be less well-off than they had expected to be—again, and not to belabor the point, this is very much like what happened with the vanishing home equity, but on a larger scale.

It can, however, also happen across a longer period of time. And this is the occasion upon which conservatives ought to remind themselves that they are conservatives, and not right-wing radicals. The changes that will come to entitlement programs and other expensive undertakings at the federal, state, and local level will be fundamental. The changes will be deep and wide. But if we move soon—and if we are lucky—we will enjoy one great luxury: the ability to make these changes slowly, piecemeal, and over a long period of time.

As Newt Gingrich once told an overzealous partisan dismayed at the slow pace of change: "Rome wasn't burned in a day." The temptation to look for a silver bullet, one-time, all-in, universal fix will be great and, if we are unlucky, it may even become necessary. But as attractive as that possibility may be, denying ourselves the pleasure of implementing it should be the main political goal of reasonable reformers in both parties and of all ideological stripes for as long as the threat of crisis remains. Crises are unruly things, and only fools and the power-mad hope for them. It is one thing to have a plan to get rich, another to have a plan to get rich *quick*. One is a strategy, the other a scheme. We should welcome the opportunity for necessary reform, but not welcome it too enthusiastically. The world isn't ending. Yet.

Under the Scientific Bo Tree

Anthony Daniels

Le métier d'homme est difficile.
— Georges Simenon, *Le neige était sale*

IN HIS MEMOIRS, Sir Arthur Conan Doyle says that the philosophy of Moleschott was all the rage when he was a medical student in Edinburgh during the late 1870s and early 1880s. Jacob Moleschott (1822–93) was a Dutch physiologist who had also studied philosophy in his youth and was a militant materialist. He is remembered today, if at all, for a couple of aphorisms that sum up his philosophy: "There is no thought without phosphorus" and "The brain secretes thought as the liver secretes bile."

I suppose it is true that, metaphorically speaking, thought can become as blocked as bile, and even more irritant in its effects. But this summary, and surely very premature, dismissal of the puzzle of human consciousness and all its associated problems did not long satisfy Conan Doyle, who perhaps went to the other extreme and came to believe in everything from spirit messages to ectoplasm and fairies at the bottom of the garden. Overall, it is not easy to say which of the pair was the more irrational, Conan Doyle or Moleschott, though it is easy to say which was the more attractive. If I had to choose, however, I should award the palm for irrationality to Moleschott because he was so unconsciously prey to the sin of pride, believing himself to have fathomed the unfathomable (give or take an experiment or two).

Of course, Moleschott was neither the first nor the last to suffer from this beguiling scientistic illusion. Some of the less self-assured among his predecessors and successors have claimed that, while there is no such realm as the unfathomable, there still remains much that is unfathomed. For some reason, however, there has been a tendency for even these more modest types to slide gradually from the belief that everything is explicable to the belief that they have explained everything (again, more or less), and that they have therefore achieved enlightenment, as it were, under the scientific bo tree.

The question of what advance in human self-understanding is to be expected from the almost exponential growth in technological sophistication is not an easy one—though perhaps it ought to be if, as is sometimes claimed, we are fast approaching such understanding. But even the question of what constitutes self-understanding is far from easy. Very often my patients would tell me that they would stop drinking to excess (or indulging in some other kind of patently self-destructive behavior) if only they understood why they did it. "What," I asked them, "would count as an explanation? Give me an example."

They were never able to do so. Their very attempts died on their lips as they made them. Was it their genes, their peculiar biochemistry, their upbringing, their drinking environment, the price of alcohol? (There is a strong inverse relationship in any society between the quantity of alcohol consumed per capita and its price.) Some algebraic combination of all these? No human being believes or can possibly believe this of himself, except perhaps for self-exculpatory purposes that he knows in his heart to be dishonest. It is possible to believe it only of others. The man who claims to understand himself in this fashion is like an army that declares victory and goes home.

Of course, intellectuals are as avid for fame and power as for truth, and deep skepticism or the acknowledgment of radical ignorance is not the way to create a following. Claims to total understanding, at least in outline, of human existence have not been lacking, most notably in the last century by Marxists and Freudians, with Behaviorists coming in a poor third. No human conduct ever puzzled a psychoanalyst, at least not for long, only until he had successfully fitted a few facts into the Procrustean bed of his theoretical presuppositions; likewise no Marxist possessed of the laws of dialectical materialism ever found any historical development surprising. And since the numbers of intellectuals in the last century desirous of a non-religious explanation of everything increased very rapidly, the number of people thinking that the heart had been plucked out of man's mystery was greater than ever before. Meanwhile, of course, men continued to behave badly and history continued to produce its surprises.

It is easy to see the attraction, or seductiveness, of what one might call Moleschottian reductionism. For example, if an elderly patient were to begin to behave in an uncharacteristic way, to experience hallucinations, act aggressively, and so forth, and the doctor discovered that his blood had a low level of sodium, the doctor would consider that the change in behavior was sufficiently explained. Restoring the level of sodium in the blood would almost certainly restore the patient's behavior to normal. Of course, the question would still arise as to why the level of sodium fell in the first place (a question that must be asked in order to restore it to its correct level), but the doctor would not waste his time on the metaphysical question of the relation of biochemistry to consciousness. He would consider merely that he had solved a problem.

Many other examples could be given. The case of Phineas Gage appears in 60 percent of psychology textbooks, and practically no popularizing work of materialism that justifies the ways of Man to Man is complete without references to it. There is even a children's book about Phineas Gage, which informs children that "what happened and what didn't happen inside the brain of Phineas Gage will tell you a lot about how your brain works and how you act human."

Phineas Gage (1823–60) was working as a foreman on railway construction in Vermont when an explosion drove an iron bar through one of the frontal lobes of his brain. Against all expectations he survived the injury and furthermore did so without obvious disablement such as paralysis of any of his limbs or an inability to speak. But according to the almost universally accepted story, Gage's personality and character underwent a dramatic change as a result of the accident. Whereas before it he had been a model citizen—sober, industrious, uxorious, and responsible—he became almost the opposite—impulsive, foulmouthed, egotistical, thoughtless, and unpredictable. His morality changed: therefore morality (or, as the book about him for children puts it, "How you act human") could be understood as a function of the frontal lobes.

Recently, this account of Gage's life has been challenged. Detailed research has shown how slight is the evidence for his almost Nietzschean transformation of his character: not more, in fact, than a few hundred words of notes written by his doctor in Vermont. Gage held down jobs subsequent to his injury that were almost incompatible with his supposed new character, but, whatever the historical truth of the matter, it is now as unlikely that he will ever be deposed from his position as the unwitting patron saint of neurosciences as it is that Saint Jude will cease to be the patron saint of lost causes.

In truth, the advances of the neurosciences of which Gage is the patron saint have been remarkable (to understate the case). Who would ever have thought it possible for the excessive gambling associated with Parkinson's disease, which is understood to be caused by the death of dopamine-secreting cells in the substantia nigra area of the brain, could sometimes be corrected by means of a surgical operation? Since excessive gambling is a moral problem par excellence, the Moleschottian consequences of this operation seem perfectly clear: The brain secretes morality as the liver secretes bile.

A recent example of what one might call the reduction of meaning to neurology is *The Science of Evil* by the psychologist Simon Baron-Cohen. Baron-Cohen is one of the greatest world experts on autism, a condition in which people, from their earliest age, do not relate to their fellow human beings normally as bearers of consciousness but as objects. It is said that, rather like behaviorists, they have no theory of mind. Baron-Cohen suggests that the term "evil" is worthless at best and harmful at worst. It has no explanatory power. We say that a person is evil because of what he does, and does what he does because he is evil. The explanandum and the explanans are one and the same. But because the term appears to be explanatory, it discourages or inhibits genuine thought about why people behave badly.

Certainly I have known instances of this error. For example, I remember the murder trial of a young man who lived in a flop-house and had beaten a fellow resident to death over the disappearance of a trifling piece of jewelry. The expert for the defense said that the accused was a psychopath, that is to say he suffered from a lifelong, quasi-neurological defect of personality that substantially reduced his responsibility for his acts. The prosecuting counsel asked the expert what evidence there was that the accused was a psychopath. The expert, a man of great eminence who had made the mistake of supposing that eminence was a substitute for thoroughness, and who expected to be believed, answered ex cathedra that, if the accused had not been a psychopath, he would not have done what he did. The prosecuting counsel asked no more questions, and the expert left the witness box sublimely unaware of his auto-destruction (eminence being the protective antibody of self-esteem).

Baron-Cohen argues that henceforth we should explain acts that in the past we would so uselessly have designated evil by reference to the lack of empathy of the person or persons who committed them. This lack of empathy is itself a condition of the brain. Not only is the capacity to empathize with human and other living beings a characteristic that, like height, exists on a continuum, with a normal or bell-shaped distribution, possibly with a genetic basis, but lack of empathy, temporary or permanent, can result from insults to the brain, like that suffered by (to take an example purely at random) Phineas Gage. It is even possible to show differences in the brain scans of the empathetic and the heartless. In other words, people who do the worst things are not so much bad as ill, whether the illness is congenital or acquired.

The practical, and far from liberal, consequences of this conception of evil (and of lesser wrongdoing) were long ago pointed out, not least by C. S. Lewis in his essay "The Humanitarian Theory of Punishment." If wrongdoing is disease, punishment is, or ought to be, its cure—and cure is a matter of fact, not of justice:

> When we cease to consider what the criminal deserves and consider only what will cure him or deter others, we have tacitly removed him from the sphere of justice altogether; instead of a person, a subject of rights, we now have a mere object, a patient, a "case."

The rights of which Lewis here speaks are not those so beloved of European politicians—tangible material benefits that impose economic obligations on others, such as six weeks' paid holidays in exotic locales—but "natural" ones, such as that not to be punished without having broken the law. But a theory, such as that human evil or wrongdoing is reducible to neurology, is not to be disposed of merely because we do not like the consequences. If it is true, it is true. The problem is that it is metaphysically naive.

Baron-Cohen accidentally gives the game away when he discusses the case of a Buddhist monk, supposed by others to be a man of more than normal empathy, who "had spent his life learning to control his reaction to his own pain and to that of others." He says that the "empathy circuits" in his brain were shown by sophisticated scanning to be "overactive" while he sat in an uncomfortable position, as presumably they were when he witnessed the suffering of others. Baron-Cohen writes:

> First, if someone can suppress their [*sic*] own pain sensations, while that might be a useful skill on the battlefield or in competitive sports, it is not clear that this is required for super-empathy. Secondly, if you suppress your *appropriate* emotional response to another person's pain, how is that empathic? Whatever the monk was doing, and it was clearly abnormal, it doesn't fit my definition of empathy.

There are two important things to notice here. The first is that the writer has previously identified areas of the brain that supposedly secrete empathy as the liver secretes bile: for when a person feels empathy, certain areas of his brain light up in the scan. Unfortunately, it does not follow from this that, when those areas light up in the scan, he feels empathy. This is precisely what Baron-Cohen finds: although the monk's empathetic brain areas light up, his state of mind cannot realistically be called empathic, not even by someone as dedicated to the neurology of empathy as Baron-Cohen.

Of course, it would be open to Baron-Cohen to argue that, as yet, brain scans are very crude, despite their superficial technological virtuosity. What they mainly show is the consumption of oxygen by various areas of the brain, it being assumed that, when an area of the brain is brought into more than ordinary use, when it is in drive position rather than in neutral or parking, it consumes more oxygen. This method is like trying to catch water vapor with a butterfly net; the number of neuronal connections in the human brain is even more astronomical, at least for the moment, than that of the national debt.

Scans *will* become more and more sophisticated, and other tools will likewise be developed. Eventually, they will be of such refinement that it will be possible to scan a person's brain and tell with certainty what he thinks or feels. I am not philosopher or logician enough to say whether this vision—or nightmare—is within the realm of possibility. The fact that the human mind is capable of generating an indefinitely large number of thoughts, expressed in an indefinitely large number of ways, each of them unique and unprecedented, would seem to me to tell against it, to make it impossible that we could ever do entirely without the subjective reports of our fellow-beings to know what they are thinking. But whether it tells against it metaphysically—that is to say a priori—as a very possibility and not just as an immensely difficult empirical feat, I leave to others to decide.

The philosophers Paul and Patricia Churchland, among others, hope that one day such retrograde and primitive expressions as Juliet's "Alack, alack, that heaven should practise stratagems/Upon so soft a subject as myself" will be replaced, or at any rate be replaceable, with purely scientific terms in a strict physico-chemical denotation. They would prefer Juliet, or that organism temporarily occupying such and such a space on stage, commonly but no doubt inaccurately known as the actress playing Juliet (because personal identity is itself part of that folk psychology that is destined for the dustbin of history), to tell us that neuronal connections 39947474747, 58883883821, and 979333002842 of the brain of the actress are now firing. Then, of course, we should know precisely what was really going on, without all that blather about heaven practicing stratagems.

Why anyone should wish this is beyond my scope to enquire, and one must always remember that the seeming perversity of a desire is not in itself evidence that a desire is unattainable. For a philosophical scheme such as the Churchlands' to work it must (it seems to me) do immense violence to normal human experience; while experience can show that any given experience is mistaken, or even that many experiences are mistaken, it cannot show, without self-contradiction, that all experience is mistaken—and that experience requires a being that experiences.

There is a second problem in the passage from Baron-Cohen that I have quoted. He writes of "appropriate emotion," but where in the physical world do we find the quality of appropriateness? I remember as a student of physiology observing the rage reaction of cats with electrodes implanted into their amygdalas, a rage that was not directed at anything in their environment, that arose merely when an electric current was passed down the electrode, and was therefore deemed "inappropriate." But the language of appropriateness and inappropriateness belongs to the world of ends and not of facts; it is only if one assumes that a cat's rage has a purpose, for example that of protecting it from a dangerous opponent, that the language has any meaning, that a rage can be inappropriate. Perhaps this is the reason why even the strictest Darwinists have such difficulty in eliminating the language of intention from their writing.

Will one ever be able to put a man's head in a scanner (or other instrument) and say, "He is now having an appropriate emotion"? And if you and I disagree as to whether his emotion is appropriate, is there conceptually any fact to which you or I could point that would settle the matter in the same way as, for example, a laboratory test might settle a diagnosis? It is possible, of course, that you might know more about him than I, that he has such and such a history behind him that causes him to react in this way, which you deem appropriate; but no number of facts could compel our agreement, even if we were committed to complete intellectual honesty as to the acceptance of facts. And if it is true that human life is literally inconceivable without judgment as to such matters as the appropriateness of emotion (to say nothing of morality and beauty), then human existence will never be reducible to a physical description of it, however sophisticated technology becomes. Whether we like it or not, we live in a world of meaning irreducible to physical processes: even if, as with some regret I believe, we are merely physical beings.

The desire of so many thinkers to deny the importance, or even the reality, of the only thing that makes human life worth living, consciousness, is surely rather a strange one. It is if a leopard were happy about everything except its spots. It is like the self-abasing rage of a frustrated megalomaniac, or a Hamlet:

> What a piece of work is a man, how noble in reason, how infinite in faculties, in form and moving how express and admirable, in action how like an angel, in apprehension how like a god! the beauty of the world, the paragon of animals— and yet, to me, what is this quintessence of dust?

If quintessence of dust we are, and to dust we must return (I remember a picture in my children's encyclopedia, dating from the 1920s, in which a man was reduced to his chemical components, a little pile of sulphur, potassium, carbon in the form of coal, phosphorus, a balloon full of oxygen, and so forth, impressive and not very impressive at the same time), perhaps it would be best, less humiliating, if we were never up to much in the first place. If consciousness is an illusion, an epiphenomenon, then to lose it by means of death is nothing to fear, but we do fear death, so consciousness is an illusion, an epiphenomenon.

The lengths to which man will go to degrade himself are remarkable. I remember reading the preface to the first edition of Richard Dawkins's historically very important book *The Selfish Gene,* written by the great evolutionary biologist Robert Trivers, in which it was claimed that research on the social bees and wasps demonstrated conclusively that there was no reason why men and women should have different roles in life. I laughed: You might as well say wives have no option but to kill and eat their husbands because some female spiders kill and eat their mates. Equality of the sexes might be right for a number of reasons, but the behavior of the social wasps is assuredly not one of them.

The light shone on human existence by Darwinism seems to me to be less than blinding. Referring to the theory of kin selection—the tendency of animals to behave in such a way as to increase the chances of reproduction of their close relatives, even at the risk of danger to themselves—the biologist J. B. S. Haldane once said jokingly that he would be prepared to die for two brothers or eight cousins. This undoubtedly captures part of the truth about human beings, that on the whole they go to much greater lengths for their children or other close relatives than for complete strangers or for those not likely ever to be in a position to reciprocate favors. But this is no more an invariable rule than is the maximization of profit of the supposed *homo oeconomicus.* Of course it is true that some people sometimes maximize their profit even if it means riding roughshod over others, but no sensible person would claim that this is an exhaustive description, much less an exhaustive explanation, of human behavior. Likewise, instances of parental neglect or disregard for the interests of their children must surely be within everyone's experience, and, to judge by natality rates in Europe, reproductive success is not by any means a universal human goal, either conscious or unconscious.

Darwinist explanations of human conduct always have an after-the-fact quality about them. They have very little predictive value and they do not help anyone to decide how to act. In *The Moonstone,* by Wilkie Collins, Betteredge, the butler, regards Robinson Crusoe as an oracular book and consults it constantly for practical guidance. It is rather difficult to imagine anyone using *The Origin of Species, The Descent of Man,* or any other work of evolutionary theory in the same way.

This is not to say that evolutionary theory is never of any explanatory or predictive power whatever. It correctly predicts, for example, that step-parents are more likely to neglect, abuse, or even kill the children with whom they live than are biological parents, the so-called Cinderella Effect (Daly and Wilson, for example, found that the homicide rate by step-fathers in Canada was 120 times that of biological fathers); this, the theory suggests, is because evolutionary pressure has selected us to be specially protective towards our biological offspring. In other words, one is programmed biologically to love one's own children in a way that one is not programmed to love other children; in certain circumstances, the demands of parenting children other than the step-parent's own will seem, consciously or unconsciously, an impediment or menace to the welfare of his own biological children.

When the objection is made that the great majority of step-parents do not kill their step-children, the Darwinists reply that their theory does not require this, only that they do so more frequently, something that has been proved to be the case across many countries and many cultures. In fact, the Cinderella Effect has been found wherever it has been looked for. Nor is it a valid objection that killing a step-child is unlikely to benefit the biological children of the killer because, in contemporary societies, he will be apprehended and incarcerated, thus depriving his children of his support. The theory does not require that evolutionary behavior should be adapted to society as it has developed, only that it should be adapted to the life of man in the wild.

Yet when we descend from the level of statistical generalities to particular cases, we feel that the theory has not explained everything, or even all that much. We want to know why step-parent A rather than step-parent X, Y, or Z killed his step-child, and to explain that we are obliged to examine his particular circumstances: his character, his habits, what he had drunk that day, etc. We would not be satisfied to be told that evolutionary theory predicted that step-parents should kill step-children more often than biological parents killed biological children, and that he had acted in fulfilment of this general law. Even when we knew everything we could know about the killer, however, we would probably not be entirely satisfied that we fully understood why he had picked up the baby and smashed its head against the wall, for nothing that we had learned about him, not one single explanatory factor or combination of explanatory factors, would be unique. There is something irreducibly individual in human conduct, and once again we are left trying to capture water vapor with a butterfly net.

In other words, even when evolutionary theory is at its most plausible, it fails to illuminate as much as its proponents suppose or would like. Not only are other explanations conceivable for what is, after all, only a very small (if dramatic) aspect of the totality of human behavior, but the very facility with which it explains the failure of most step-parents to kill—that by nurturing step-children to a certain extent, they are ensuring their sexual access to the mother—has an unmistakable aura of glibness about it. And, once again, it does violence to human experience to say that the innumerable step-parents who have loved their step-children as their own have done so only because they were particularly anxious to secure their own sexual access to the mother.

Darwinism as the latest substitute for religion for those who seek religious meaning without being religious (the previous two being Marxism and Freudianism) is clearly illustrated in an article in a recent edition of the *British Medical Journal,* written by two professors, one from

New Zealand and the other from America. Titled "Evolutionary Biology Within Medicine: A Perspective of Growing Value," it ends:

> Evolutionary explanations may offer the patient valuable insights into their condition: "Why is this happening to me? Why is my body letting me down?" Science, through an understanding of our evolutionary history and the evolutionary processes that constructed our physiology, will come closest to answering the question, "What does it mean to be a human organism?"

If this kind of scientistic vacuity were not on the way to becoming an unassailable orthodoxy in some circles, to be taught as Truth in medical schools, it would be funny. Human organism indeed! Human organism describes me about as well as did the term human resource for the hospital in which I once worked.

The best example, because by far the most plausible, that the authors can offer the reader is that of the development and spread of microbial resistance to antibiotics, a subject of great interest to practicing doctors. On such a subject, evolutionary theory can be expected to be truly illuminating, but to liken the complexities of human existence to the development of microbial resistance is about as illuminating as likening a foxhole to Versailles.

SCIENCE AND TECHNOLOGY undoubtedly change us, though not necessarily in the direction of increased self-understanding or depth of character. To take one small example from myself, the case that I should know best and upon which I ought to be some kind of authority: I spent quite a lot of my earlier life in such remote places that I was for weeks or months out of communication with my friends or anybody who might want to contact me,

whereas I now begin to grow anxious—a little anxious—
if I am separated from telephonic or email communication
for more than an hour or two. This, I suspect, is not
merely a progression in the stage of my life that would
have happened anyway, but a change wrought by something external to me. Those who, unlike me, have grown
up with all the media of superficial communication experience anxiety when separated from them from an early
age.

Recently, I attended a conference in which American
researchers presented evidence that American children
now spend, on average, seven hours a day in front of one
kind of screen or another (and there is no reason why children elsewhere should be any different, at least not for
long). Some spent as many as sixteen hours in front of
screens; some scarcely ever met, let alone spoke to, their
parents, so absorbed were they by or in their screens. In
Britain, a child is considerably more likely to have a television in his bedroom than a father living at home.

The researchers found that children who spent the
most time in front of screens were the most maladjusted
socially and educationally—not a surprising finding, perhaps, but the researchers had not done enough work yet
to decide in which direction the causation, if any, flowed.
They ran two interesting experiments. In the first, they
generated signals at random intervals to a group of children's mobile telephones, asking the children to use their
phones when they received such a signal to video the
room in which they were currently placed. Often it
showed the children attending to several screens at once,
with multiple sources of electronic sensory stimulus at the
same time, often while they were doing their homework.
In the second experiment, they asked a group of children
to forgo all forms of electronic communication for two

weeks. At first they were reluctant to do so, saying that life would be completely impossible without them, that their social lives would quite literally come to an end in the absence of email, phones, Facebook, and Twitter. Nevertheless, the group agreed to try, and, at the end of the two weeks, they not only felt the happier for it, but that their lives had been enriched, not impoverished, by the absence of all the paraphernalia. As soon as the two weeks were up, however, they returned to their apparatus as an addict to his drug, though they expected no good to come of the return.

Has the proliferation of electronic means of communication altered human character in any basic way, such that a new self-understanding is necessary? Has the human personality been hollowed out by too-facile and habitual contact in the virtual world? When I made myself incommunicado for months on end, I had no doubt whatever that my friendships were strong enough to resume exactly where they had left off when I returned, and so it proved, but I wonder whether in an age of Facebook, when so much communication seems based upon a tacit understanding that I will pretend that your trivia is interesting if you will pretend that mine is too, such friendships as those I formed early in my life that could survive prolonged absence are still formed, or even formable?

In similar vein, I wonder whether attention spans of more than a few moments can ever develop in an environment in which fast moving images so preoccupy minds for what amount in total to years of waking time? And without the power to concentrate, without the awareness even that it is necessary to concentrate, without the ability to sit still and attend to the motions of our own minds (as Dr. Johnson puts it), are we condemned to superficiality?

How can those qualities necessary to pursue, if never finally to achieve, self-understanding ever arise, where the most important written communication between people takes its name from the vociferations of small birds?

Perhaps these are just the thoughts of someone who, though he uses and has benefited enormously from the new communication technologies, at heart dislikes them, and sees in them what old people are apt to see in all change, the devaluation of their own past and the supercession of what they have most liked about existence. And certainly I meet enough young people of high attainment and depth of character to persuade me that all is not lost, indeed that, underneath the hallucinating changes, everything fundamental about human existence—love, joy, hope, despair, puzzlement, mortality—remains the same, untouched by neuroscience, evolutionary theory, or Twitter.

And this in turn means that attempts at human self-understanding, by the means of art, philosophy, and science, will neither cease nor achieve final triumph. Technical and existential progress will remain forever unconnected. There will always be more than enough mystery to thwart those who claim to know, at long last, "how you act human," and "what it means to be a human organism."

What's a Museum?

James Panero

However perplexing the problems of the present and the future, however sobering the obligations laid upon the museums of America through the destruction of war, the past gives confidence for the days to come.
— Winifred E. Howe, *A History of the Metropolitan Museum of Art,* 1946

WHAT'S A MUSEUM? Lately, it seems, the answer is whatever we want. Today's museums can be tourist attractions, department stores, civic centers, town squares, catalysts of urban renewal, food courts, licensing brands, showcases for contemporary architecture, social clubs, LEED-certified environmentally conscious facilities, and franchise opportunities. A "well-run museum is eerily like an upscale suburban shopping mall," says an article in *The New York Times.* A cafe with "art on the side," advertises London's Victoria and Albert Museum. "We are in the entertainment business, and competing against other forms of entertainment out there," says a one-time spokesman for the Guggenheim museum. "Inclusive places that welcome diverse audiences" and "reflect our society's pluralism in every aspect of their operations and programs," suggests the American Association of Museums. "We live in a more global, multicultural society that cares about diversity and inclusivity," as "service to the community" is now among the museum's à la carte options, says Kaywin Feldman, the latest head of the Association of Art Museum Directors. As reported in *The Wall Street Journal,* museums are even about "bringing art to those with Alzheimer's or post-traumatic stress disorder, and farming crops for donation to local food banks," initiatives that have been promoted through grants from the National Endowment for the Arts.

By the numbers, today's museums are thriving enterprises. Billions of dollars have been spent in recent years on expansion projects. In the United States, there were 46 art museums in 1905, 60 in 1910, and 387 in 1938. Today there are 3,500 art museums, more than half of them founded after 1970, and 17,000 museums of all types in total, including science museums, children's museums, and historical houses. Attendance at American art museums is booming, rising from 22 million a year in 1962 to over 100 million in 2000, with 850 million Americans visiting museums of all varieties each year.

Yet if today's museums are successful cultural caterers with wide-ranging menus, no matter where we find them, their fare manages to taste more and more the same. A handful of the same celebrity architects now designs new wings and even whole museum cities such as Saadiyat Island in Abu Dhabi. Facilities in Spain, Boston, the Middle East, and Los Angeles all look different in the same way. An international class of museum professionals job-hops among Beijing, Paris, New York, and Qatar spreading a common corporate culture, where top directors are expected to command million-dollar salaries, oversee thousands of employees, fund-raise, invest and spend endowments on massive expansions, horse-trade the assets on the walls to create blockbuster shows that can attract headline-making crowds, and spin these activities to the press.

Is all this hyperactivity the glow of health or the flush of fever? Philippe de Montebello, the former director of The Metropolitan Museum of Art, suggests the latter. With yesterday's art traded away for today's trends, exhibition halls taken over by "social space," and new buildings expanding around traditional facilities, museums are shedding their old skin and remaking themselves in our image. It is said that museums have gone from "being about something" to "being for somebody." "The work of art, once sovereign, has ceded primacy of place in many an administration's attention to the public," de Montebello lamented in a lecture at Harvard, published in the book *Whose Muse? Art Museums and the Public Trust*. Museums have traditionally been focused on their permanent collections. By emphasizing the visitor, museums now risk forsaking the visited and their own cultural importance. Museums were once the arks of culture. Now the artifacts at greatest risk may be themselves.

"Prosperity is a great teacher," wrote William Hazlitt, but "adversity is a greater." The story of London's National Gallery in wartime offers up a poignant lesson about the historical relationship between museums and their permanent collections, and the lengths that nations will go to save them.

During the Second World War, Kenneth Clark, The National Gallery's young director, needed to get his institution's collection of European paintings out from under the Luftwaffe's bomb sites. As recounted in Suzanne Bosman's 2008 book *The National Gallery in Wartime*, Clark was right about the threat to the collection in central London. Between October 1940 and April 1941,

Nazi nighttime aerial bombardment struck The National Gallery nine times. On October 12, 1940, a German explosive leveled what had been the Raphael room.

At first Clark removed the Gallery's holdings from Trafalgar Square to a discrete handful of universities, libraries, and castles scattered across Wales and Gloucestershire. When Germany inaugurated its Liverpool Blitz and Nazi bombers came within striking distance of these temporary homes, Clark prepared an even more drastic contingency. He was aware of the U-Boat menace. Nevertheless, he drew up plans to ship the permanent collection off the British Isles to the safety of Canada.

When Clark approached Winston Churchill about the move, the Prime Minister had a better idea. "Hide them in caves and cellars," Churchill declared by telegram, "but not one picture shall leave this island." Churchill's remarks signaled the importance of The National Gallery and, in particular, its permanent collection to the identity of the nation. A work of art may exist in isolation, but a culture of art lives through museums and the collections these museums have maintained for the public. These permanent collections embody a museum's identity even more than its buildings, its record of traveling shows, or any other aspect of its operations. Clark wanted to save the works of art. Churchill saw that Britain needed to preserve its culture of art as well. Sending away the art might spare the canvases, but it would mean disrupting the permanence of the permanent collection.

In 1941, Clark found a way to honor Churchill's determination. First he reunited the scattered collection by retrofitting an abandoned slate mine into an air-conditioned storage facility. A year later, he began bringing the collection back to The National Gallery through the "Picture of the Month" initiative.

In January of that year, a letter published in the *Times* of London signed by a "picture-lover" wondered if there could be a way to bring the treasures of the permanent collection back on public view. "Because London's face is scarred and bruised these days," the writer suggested, "we need more than ever to see beautiful things." Clark devised a way to bring up one masterpiece from the slate mine and exhibit it temporarily on Trafalgar Square. By night, and during daytime air raids, Clark moved the painting to a strong room in the basement. The first masterpiece to see the wartime walls was *Margaretha de Geer,* a work attributed to Rembrandt purchased by the Gallery in 1941 but, until then, never placed on public view. Even with severe limitations on travel, Clark calculated that as many visitors came to see that one painting each day as would have visited the entire National Gallery on a day in peacetime.

Clark chose the next painting—the first official "Picture of the Month"—by reading the suggestions that poured into his offices at the Gallery. The top request, he discovered, was Titian's *Noli Me Tangere.* The painting depicts Mary Magdalene reaching out towards Christ after the resurrection, who tells her, "Touch me not; for I am not yet ascended to my father." "Almost certainly it was not the historical or physical truths of the picture that really mattered, but its poetic truth," notes Neil MacGregor, the director of The National Gallery from 1987 to 2002. These pictures are not solitary objects but the visual bonds of a nation. They "exist to enable the public to explore through them their own personal and shared experience, as generations have done before us and will do in the future."

The art critic Herbert Read, writing during the war, declared The National Gallery to be "a defiant outpost of culture right in the middle of a bombed and shattered metropolis." At the conclusion of hostilities in 1945, Clark ensured the swift return of the entire collection to Trafalgar Square. The rehanging of the paintings became a cause for national celebration. As a reporter for the *Observer* concluded at the time, "The National Gallery is far more genuinely a national possession than ever before."

From its founding, The National Gallery, like all great museums, has meant more than the sum of its parts, however magnificent. Leo von Klenze, who designed several institutions throughout Munich in the first half of the nineteenth century, including the Glyptothek, called the modern museum "one of the truly living ideals of this age."

The identity of The National Gallery is not found on a balance sheet but through an intangible idea tied to a collection held and displayed in the public trust. Since this museum was created when the House of Commons purchased the picture collection of the banker John Julius Angerstein for the nation in 1824, The National Gallery, which opened on Trafalgar Square in 1838, has from the start represented a British ideal of parliamentary government. Unlike many of the other museums in Europe, with their permanent collections nationalized from other pre-existing institutions, the collection of The National Gallery was purchased on behalf of the British people by their lawful representatives. To have sent away The National Gallery's collection in wartime would have meant sending away a manifestation of British self-rule. The masterpieces that came on view through Clark's "Picture of the Month" initiative were not merely Rembrandts and Titians, but the Rembrandts and Titians of The National Gallery, of Parliament, and of the British people.

The great museums of the West, founded mainly between the late eighteenth and late nineteenth centuries, have almost all functioned like The National Gallery to represent the characteristic ideals of their nations, almost always through an identity intimately connected to their permanent collections.

The Louvre was founded in 1793 to represent the French Revolution through the nationalized treasures seized from the monarchy, the church, and later colonial conquest, all to be exhibited in a seized Bourbon palace. The Prado Museum, which Ferdinand VII opened to the public in 1819 as the Royal Museum of Paintings and Sculptures, represented the last sparkles of beauty from the fading Spanish Crown. The Hermitage Museum, founded by Catherine the Great in 1764 and opened to the public in 1852, represented Russian imperial power through its ability to import great art from the West. After 1917, when many masterpieces of its permanent collection were sent into storage like locked-up dissidents, the Hermitage became a manifestation of totalitarian state control.

The many museums that emerged in Germany in the nineteenth century mainly sought out a spiritual ideal. Friedrich Hölderlin saw museums as "aesthetic churches," where the artists are the anointed priests. The Prussian architect Karl Friedrich Schinkel, who called museums temples of art, applied neoclassical elements to his designs. Schinkel's museums served to recast the royal patrimonies of their collections into art in the public trust after the work was, for a time, nationalized by Napoleonic France. The pillared porticos like those on Berlin's Altes (Old) Museum, known as the Royal Museum when it opened in 1830, also turned his buildings into latter-day Greek temples. The soaring entrances of Schinkel's museums were meant as places where, as he put it, "the individual could recollect himself and prepare himself for the mysteries that awaited him; it was not to be a social place, but rather a place where the individual divorced himself from society."

The close association of European museums and their permanent collections with national ideals was underscored by their ownership, which to this day almost always remains some form of government control. Britain's National Gallery, for example, describes its governing structure as a "non-departmental public body, whose sponsor body is the Department for Culture, Media and Sport," with a board of trustees appointed primarily by the Prime Minister.

In the United States, the same cannot be said of comparable institutions. American museums began to propagate a generation later than their European counterparts as an answer to those institutions, yet with a key difference that is so apparent it is often overlooked. American museums vary widely in their missions, but they almost all share a similar story as institutions founded and supported by private individuals. Today, most of them remain not-for-profit institutions largely supported through private donations.

Their private status might seem to preclude the association of American museums with a national identity, but the lack of government ownership in fact goes to the heart of their own ideal. It may seem that the philanthropy supporting American museums is ancillary to the treasures the institutions contain. But those treasures, however singular, are also tokens of the idealism behind the institutions that maintain them.

As manifestations of private wealth transferred to the public trust, American museums were founded, in part, to represent virtue. The visual education offered to the

public by these museums through their permanent collections is not just an education in art history but also a
lesson in how individual hard work can become an expression of virtue by giving over objects of beauty to the public trust. No other country has seen such private wealth,
accumulated through industry, willingly transferred to the
public good. Even as institutions around the world now
attempt to supplement their own government funding
with private support on the American model, the philanthropic culture of the United States remains a singular
phenomenon. The countless "American Friends of ..."
groups that now exist for cultural institutions around the
globe are testament to America's continued abundance of
philanthropic energies.

Virtue in both private and public life was of primary
concern to the American Founders, who along with education and the rule of law included virtue among the
foundations of freedom. "'Tis substantially true that
virtue or morality is a necessary spring of popular government," George Washington said in his Farewell Address.
Or as John Adams wrote in a letter to Mercy Otis Warren
in 1776: "Public Virtue cannot exist in a Nation without
private, and public Virtue is the only Foundation of
Republics. There must be a positive Passion for the public
good, the public Interest, Honour, Power and Glory,
established in the Minds of the People, or there can be
no Republican Government, nor any real Liberty."

The American museum consciously emerged out of
this ideal of self-governance, a belief that a virtuous people
with a passion for the public good might create institutions in the public interest that could one day rival or even
exceed the museums of Europe, all without the compulsion of government. Among the many philanthropic pur-
suits of the American public, the American art museum

has received particular attention because its treasures serve as tangible manifestations of virtue.

New York's Metropolitan Museum of Art became the first of three great encyclopedic museums to open its doors in the United States within a decade of each other. Founded in 1870 and opened in 1872, it was closely followed by The Museum of Fine Arts, Boston in 1876 (also founded in 1870) and the Philadelphia Museum of Art in 1877 (founded in 1876)—institutions that were quite different from the ones we know today but nonetheless born out of a similar philanthropic urge. As recounted in Winifred E. Howe's two-volume *History of the Metropolitan Museum of Art,* published in 1913 and 1946, the Met's founding generation emerged out of the destruction of the Civil War to speak in bold terms about the virtues of their creation. They directly connected their new museum with the ideals of a reunited nation. In 1866, John Jay gave a speech at a party of his fellow countrymen at the Pré Catalan in Paris celebrating the ninetieth anniversary of national independence. "It was time for the American people to lay the foundation of a National Institution and Gallery of Art," he urged. A committee of men formed on the spot to pursue the idea back in New York.

In 1869, with Jay as president of the Union League Club, an institution that had strongly supported the Union cause in the Civil War, the club's Art Committee issued a report that had widespread implications for the future of art:

> It will be said that it would be folly to depend upon our governments, either municipal or national, for judicious support or control in such an institution; for our governments, as a rule, are utterly incompetent for the task.... An amply

endowed, thoroughly constructed art institution, free alike from bungling government officials and from the control of a single individual, whose mistaken and untrained zeal may lead to superficial attempts and certain failures; an institution which will command the confidence of judicious friends of art, and especially of those who have means to strengthen and increase its value to the city and to the nation, is surely worth consideration in a club like this.

So that this consideration would not be confined to the Union League alone, the club sent invitations to members of the city's other thriving private clubs and art academies to join the discussion. Three hundred people turned out for a meeting at the Union League, then on Twenty-sixth Street.

Few of them were as central to the culture of nineteenth-century New York as William Cullen Bryant. The editor of the *New York Evening Post* and a member of the Union League, he became the outspoken leader of the initiative for a new art museum. Bryant Park, in back of the main branch of the New York Public Library, bears his name. Bryant never expected government to fund the Metropolitan. In fact, he expected the private philanthropy behind the institution to repudiate big government. This assurance of purpose was unmistakable when Bryant addressed the conference at the Union League:

> Our city is the third great city of the civilized world. Our republic has already taken its place among the great powers of the earth; it is great in extent, great in population, great in the activity and enterprise of her people. It is the richest nation in the world, if paying off an enormous national debt with a rapidity unexampled in history be any proof of riches; the richest in the world, if contented submission to heavy

taxation be a sign of wealth; the richest in the world, if quietly to allow itself to be annually plundered of immense sums by men who seek public stations for their individual profit be a token of public prosperity. My friends, if a tenth part of what is every year stolen from us in this way, in the city where we live, under pretence of the public service, and poured profusely into the coffers of political rogues, were expended on a Museum of Art, we might have, reposited in spacious and stately buildings, collections formed of works left by the world's greatest artists, which would be the pride of our country.

The aim of the Met's founders was not only to found a museum in New York, but also to inspire like-minded philanthropy across the country. "The other cities will follow rapidly in the wake of New York in this movement," predicted the art historian George Fisk Comfort, and he was right. Speaking at the Union League, Comfort furthermore advocated an encyclopedic museum "to represent the History of Art in all countries and in all ages of art both pure and applied."

After the New York State legislature granted the Met its Act of Incorporation in 1870, by the first decade of the twentieth century the institution was already far along building out the massive beaux-arts treasury we now find on Fifth Avenue and enriching it with a singular permanent collection—a private institution on public land. One reason for the Met's rapid ascent was the financier J. P. Morgan. His virtuous role in the cultural institutions across the city inspired New York society. A member of the Union League, Morgan was an original subscriber to The Metropolitan in 1870, became a trustee in 1888, and assumed the board presidency in 1904. "That a man known universally for his acumen in finance," writes

Winifred Howe, "should devote both time and talent to the active administration of a museum of art placed such institutions on a new footing. Other men of affairs decided that art was worthy of their attention, even their collecting, and the Museum deserving of their support."

In a memorial tribute after his death in 1913, The Metropolitan issued a resolution that took particular note of Morgan's virtue and spoke directly to his qualities of patriotic citizenship:

> He loved all forms of beauty, and with his largeness of nature and of means he became the greatest art collector of his time, and in the history of art his name must always rank with those great princes of the Old World who in former centuries protected and encouraged genius. He was as unselfish with his treasures of art as he was with his fortune. He believed that the happiness of a whole people can be increased through the cultivation of taste, and he strongly desired to contribute to that end among his own countrymen.

Looking back on the history of the Metropolitan Museum of Art in 1946, its president William Church Osborn noted that "New York owes its museum of art to the public-spirited interest of some of its citizens." He also urged his generation to "fix with sureness the philosophic and economic principles underlying all such institutions, since rapidly changing social and economic conditions are certain to bring about in the future a great need for understanding and continued study of these principles."

Osborn's urging was prescient. The assuredness of American museums through the first decades of the twentieth century, rooted in the virtues of their founders and supporters, gave way to a creeping professionalism that, in the name of good business and "best practices," sought to strip the institutions of their virtuous past.

A new bottom-line sensibility that aimed to maximize revenues and attendance numbers cut against the founding principles of American museums. "When art museums rush to be commercial or seek to titillate their visitors we see a lamentable failure of nerve," says de Montebello, who went against the grain of this professionalized museum culture as director of the Metropolitan. "Our institutions—even though often founded by businessmen in league with civic officials—were not created to make money and vaunt civic identity."

This failure of nerve is especially apparent in cases of deaccession, where institutions have justified turning their permanent collections into chattel that can be sold for profit. Among the earliest uses of the term "deaccession" was in 1972. *The New York Times* art critic John Canaday wrote that the Metropolitan Museum of Art, then under the direction of Thomas Hoving, "recently deaccessioned (the polite term for 'sold') one of its only four Redons."

Hoving was the first museum custodian to conceive of his permanent collection as a ready source of capital. In 1970, he purchased a Velázquez portrait for $5.5 million but lacked the funds to cover it. He began looking for works to sell, and the bequest of the late Adelaide de Groot was his principal target. Against the heiress's wishes that her collection remain in the institution, Hoving sold off masterpieces from her donation—most notably *The Tropics* by Henri Rousseau—through Marlborough Gallery. The sale was so controversial that the Met's curator of European painting refused to sign the deaccession form. Hoving signed it for him.

Even as the Metropolitan under de Montebello, Hoving's successor, rejected this legacy of affronting virtue, Hoving's ideas infected museum culture. Granted, by narrowing or "refining" a collection through deaccession, a museum can perform a valuable function. It can free up work from storage that may be second-rate or repetitive. A museum can raise money in a restricted endowment from the sale, to be used for the purchase of art that might better serve its mission. Peer-review organizations such as the Association of Art Museum Directors issue guidelines that, at least on paper, restrict these practices in line with traditional standards. The AAMD forbids museums, for example, from using the sale of art in their permanent collections to pay for general operating expenses or to underwrite loans. Such rules are designed to prevent museums from treating their art collections as ATM machines and sources of fast money.

But museums have been finding ways around AAMD, even as this association finds subtle ways to relax its own rules. Museums have claimed, for example, that the art in their permanent collections suddenly does not fit their mission statements, even if the work has been on display for generations. Museums use deaccession to "trade up" their permanent collections, liquidating the symbols of donor virtue while creating a slush fund for their own acquisitions. Museums have decided that certain works are of secondary importance because they are rarely shown, although this record of exhibition may merely reflect the taste of the curators.

If a museum is defined by its permanent collection, then any exhibiting institution with a permanent collection is a type of museum, even if it calls itself something different. Yet museums now routinely declare themselves to be something else just to get around the rules of AAMD, disregarding the spirit of virtue these rules represent.

One of the worst acts of deaccession occurred against the legacy of none other than William Cullen Bryant, the great advocate of the Metropolitan Museum. At the start of the twentieth century, Bryant's daughter gave *Kindred Spirits,* Asher B. Durand's 1849 Hudson River School masterpiece depicting Bryant and Thomas Cole standing at Kaaterskill Falls, to the permanent collection of the New York Public Library. In 2005, Paul LeClerc, the president of the Library, sold the painting for a $35-million payday. Even after exhibiting *Kindred Spirits* for decades, the Library claimed it was not a museum and therefore free to sell the painting for cash. The LeClerc sale was a direct affront to the founding generation of New York's cultural institutions and a demonstration of how his professional class could subvert the ideals of virtue at will.

The sale also inspired others. Two years later, Thomas Jefferson University, a medical school in Philadelphia, announced plans to sell one of the most recognizable paintings in the United States, Thomas Eakins's *The Gross Clinic* (1875), for $68 million unless a local institution could match the price within forty-five days. (The Philadelphia Museum and the Pennsylvania Academy ending up splitting the bill.)

In 2006 the Albright-Knox Art Gallery sold $71 million of its collection of older art in order to buy contemporary work, claiming the older art did not fit its mission statement. In 2008 the National Academy Museum in New York sold two valuable Hudson River School paintings to fill a budget gap, proclaiming its primary status as an art school. In 2009, the trustees of Brandeis University announced plans to shut down the school's Rose Art Museum and sell off the entire collection to raise general revenue. All the while, countless other institutions have worked under the radar to liberate their permanent collections from the restrictions imposed (as they see it) by the outdated mores of their donors.

While the profit motive drives the businesses that fund philanthropy, the perceived profiteering of American museums breaks a covenant they have made with the public and damages the culture of virtue that continues to sustain them. Sometimes this is done consciously, as museum professionals attack the past from within. At other times these professionals do damage with the best intentions. Any museum decision that appears to capitalize on the permanent collection—from gift shops to high ticket prices to fancy restaurants to facility rentals—risks diminishing the museum's virtue in the eyes of the public. What most museum professionals fail to recognize is that the principle of virtue means that good business often becomes bad business once inside the gates of these institutions.

Headline-making cases of deaccession are only the most extreme perversions of America's museum ideal, because they strike at the very embodiments of virtue. Most of today's museums therefore acknowledge that their collections maintain some special status, at least in the eyes of a reactionary public. They have learned that deaccessioning can invite unwanted publicity. So rather than go after the collections themselves, museums will more often update the facilities that contain them in order to recast or cover over the virtuous meaning of the objects inside.

Today the American Museum of Natural History, founded in 1869, is a rare holdout of traditional museum culture. Its awesome display of cultural confidence begins with James Earle Fraser's equestrian statue of Theodore Roosevelt riding through a triumphal arch at its front entrance. This foregrounds a soaring lobby designed by John Russell Pope in 1936 after Roman baths—a notably civic model compared with the more religious classicism of Germany's museums. The same sense of veneration is applied to the facilities within. Bold signs throughout the institution proclaim the donors of specimens, all without a postmodern preamble about the misuse of taxidermy. Artisans are still trained to preserve the animal models and diorama rooms of the biologist Carl Akeley, who died on assignment for the museum at the spot now depicted in the gorilla diorama. The Hall of Northwest Coast Indians has been left primarily as Franz Boas, the great anthropologist, designed it at the turn of the last century. A refurbishment of this hall that could restore its original windows, uncover its columns, and elevate the lighting would easily bring this room back to its inaugural splendor. Ten years ago, the original architecture of the fourth-floor dinosaur rooms was similarly uncovered in a brilliant restoration sponsored by David H. Koch.

There was a time, however, when this museum was far less assured of its past. In the 1940s, the institution's fanciful Romanesque Seventy-seventh-Street facade, designed by J. C. Cady in pink granite dotted with turrets and globes, was to be wiped out with the application of a monolithic slab that the critic Christopher Gray likened to "some gigantic crematorium." This new look represented the new faceless sense of what museums suddenly were supposed to be—museums without histories.

What saved this museum? In part the AMNH came to see its own history as an object worthy of protection and study. It also got lucky, undergoing budget cuts right before the wrecking ball arrived. Today the museum seems more dedicated than any other to polishing up its past and celebrating its own history along with the history of its permanent collection.

Many other institutions have been far less fortunate. The Brooklyn Museum, designed by McKim, Mead & White, lost its grand outdoor Met-like staircase to the rhetoric of "public access" in the 1930s, when the entrance was brought down to street level, the stairs ripped out, and a lobby carved out of the original auditorium. This loss created an architectural imbalance that has only been aggravated through the recent addition of a $63-million glass atrium. In the 1950s, the museum's beaux-arts lobby was similarly stripped of its ornamentation and a drop-ceiling installed. All of these moves were designed to conceal, reinterpret, or destroy the museum's one-time architectural grandeur and patrimony.

Today's museum capital projects often follow a similar pattern. With the addition of new materials, new restaurant spaces, new entertainment venues, and new contemporary art galleries designed by celebrity architects, they can be particularly seductive. The new 70,000-square-foot $114-million wing of the Isabella Stewart Gardner Museum, which opened on January 19, is but the latest. Designed by Renzo Piano, the new facility offers "purpose-built spaces for concerts, exhibitions, and classes, along with enhanced visitor amenities," according to the museum's press office, including a "cube-shaped performance hall and an adjustable height special exhibition gallery," a visitor welcome area called the "Richard E. Floor Living Room," apartments for artists-in-residence, a store called "Gift at the Gardner," a greenhouse, and a restaurant called "Café G."

The building, which required the demolition of Gardner's historic carriage house, now serves as the only entrance to the institution and connects with the original museum through a glass-enclosed umbilical cord, which penetrates the back of Gardner's fanciful Venetian building.

Compared to Gardner's grand pastiche of a museum and the limitations imposed through her trust, the Piano addition is ostentatiously invisible, obsequiously deferential, and more than willing to cater to the creature comforts of the visitor/end-user. The vertiginous theater-in-the-square turns the spectator into a spectacle. The Kunsthalle for new art, the eateries, shops, and apartments are all sumptuously attractive. A "geothermal well system, daylight harvesting, water-efficient landscaping techniques, and the use of local and regional materials" may make the new building eligible for LEED gold certification.

But what has been lost in the shuffle? How will this facility affect Gardner's original vision and the mysteries of her creation? And if the new building is meant merely as an engine to generate new donors, couldn't the trustees just as easily apply $114 million directly to the preservation of the original facility (where the water stains of a rusted-out skylight continue to streak down the interior walls)?

In countless cases, the concern is that museum professionals have come to regard their founding generations with suspicion rather than reverence. They question the legacy of these industrialists and "robber barons." They suppress the American idiosyncrasies of their institutions to appeal to international ideals. They undercut the signs of private philanthropy in order to seek out greater state control. They advance a new populist rhetoric that trumpets appeal and "access" over beauty and virtue. They attack their own "imposing" facilities and "elite" permanent collections. They undermine the art and architecture their supporters had given to the public trust. All along they sell their own expanding ranks and bureaucratic sensibilities to a complicit donor base as a way to counter, conceal, update, and "reinterpret" the influence of their museums' dubious histories.

But what if museums were to see these histories as something worthy of preservation and reverence? Some institutions have already taken such a turn. The Frick Collection, The Metropolitan Museum of Art, and the American Museum of Natural History are three of the institutions that have quietly rejected the spiraling demands of the professionalized museum by cultivating their own founding principles.

What if all American museums were to embrace the virtuous intent of their founders and supporters? The answer is that the American people, once again, could become the connoisseurs of virtue.

Enter Totalitarian Democracy

Andrew C. McCarthy

"I WOULD NOT LOOK to the U.S. Constitution if I were drafting a constitution in the year 2012." The speaker was Associate Justice Ruth Bader Ginsburg of the United States Supreme Court. These, therefore, were astonishing words.

The authority over American law enjoyed by Justice Ginsburg and her colleagues on the Court owes solely to the existence of the U.S. Constitution, complemented by the high court's proclamation that it has the last word on how that Constitution is to be construed. That latter power grab traces its roots back to Chief Justice John Marshall's legendary 1803 opinion in *Marbury v. Madison*. Marshall "emphatically" declared it "the duty of the Judicial Department to say what the law is." Despite naysayers from Jefferson to Lincoln, who thought that judicial supremacy would eviscerate popular sovereignty, Marshall's assertion paved the way for the modern Court to claim even more boldly, in *Cooper v. Aaron* (1959) for instance, that judicial control over the Constitution's meaning is a "permanent and indispensable feature of our constitutional system."

In short, were there no Constitution, there would be precious little interest in Justice Ginsburg's views. Yet, when she looks at this venerable source of her power—ratified in 1788 and, thus, as she explained, "the oldest written constitution still in force in the world"—she sees obsolescence. In its place, the Court's senior progressive ideologue advised the assemblage of university students whom she was addressing to "look at the constitution of South Africa. That was a deliberate attempt to have a fundamental instrument of government that embraced basic human rights, [and] had an independent judiciary."

But wait. Let's put aside the fact that no jurists in the world are more autonomous than the federal judges of the United States. Does not America's fundamental law, with its robust Bill of Rights addendum, embrace basic human rights? Well, no. It embraces basic human *freedoms*. That makes all the difference.

Freedom is of minimal interest to progressives, certainly not *freedom* as is commonly understood: namely, the bedrock conceit that we are our own governors, autonomous over our own lives. To be clear, we are talking about freedom in a democracy, not an anarchy. In a rational social compact, freedom requires that we surrender a quantum of our independence to secure the nation and to honor the rudimentary norms of respect for life and property. If a free society is to flourish, nothing less than ordered liberty will do.

Alas, the "liberty" part of ordered liberty is not the concern of Justice Ginsburg and her fellow travelers. For them, the individual's freedom is a relic of a bygone time, when life was simpler and dominated by sexist, slave-holding white men of a colonialist bent. The modern Left's métier is *rights,* in the contemporary connotation: i.e., what you must give to me, with government handling both the confiscation and redistribution ends of the arrangement. In contrast to the traditional rights Justice

Ginsburg finds so unrefined—to wit, the right to be free from government demands and the right to have government restricted to its expressly enumerated powers—the new rights cover everything from the mortgage arrears of spendthrifts for houses they could not afford to contraceptives for the sexual recreation of young women at nominally Catholic law schools.

On those sorts of "rights," the U.S. Constitution never was much good. Better to go with South Africa or, as Ginsburg further recommended, the Canadian Charter of Rights and Freedoms, the European Convention on Human Rights, and "all the constitution writing that has gone on since the end of World War II."

What has actually gone on since the end of World War II is the rise of "totalitarian democracy," to borrow the lapidary descriptor of the political scientist Jacob Leib Talmon. This is a form of "political Messianism" (another Talmon coinage) that must be distinguished from quaint old liberal democracy. Indeed, while the burden of this essay is to consider the place of the *rule of law* in an age of upheaval, it would be as apt to speak of the *role of law*. For what we will experience as "law" will be very different depending on which variety of democracy remains when the upheaval's dust has settled.

The totalitarian democratic school, Talmon instructed, "is based upon the assumption of a sole and exclusive truth in politics." Liberal democracy, by contrast, "assumes politics to be a matter of trial and error." It takes human beings as basically good but incorrigibly fallible, and sees their political systems as just another pragmatic contrivance in lives that for the most part are lived "altogether outside the sphere of politics." To the contrary, the avatars of totalitarian democracy maintain that they have arrived at a sole and exclusive truth. Consequently, the personal becomes the political. The car you drive, the clothes you wear, and the movies you watch—it all becomes, as President Barack Obama is fond of saying, a "teachable moment." Politics is not on the sideline; it is the juggernaut that perfects mankind in accordance with the totalitarian truth. Law is the principal instrument by which this overwhelming force is wielded.

As such, law manifests the central contradiction of political Messianism. Totalitarian democrats, also known as "progressives," have feigned homage to the centrality of freedom since the French Revolution. But whereas the conservative (i.e., the classic, Burkean "liberal") finds the essence of freedom in what Talmon described as "spontaneity and the absence of coercion," progressives like Justice Ginsburg and President Barack Obama "believe it to be realized only in the pursuit and attainment of an absolute collective purpose."

Thus, the circle that cannot be squared: Even if we assume for the sake of argument that totalitarian democrats are well-intentioned—that their quest for social justice, their "absolute collective purpose," is not merely a thin veneer for the pursuit of raw power—human freedom is not compatible with an exclusive pattern of social existence. Thinking that it *is* leads to cognitive dissonance of the Jean-Jacques Rousseau variety. Rousseau was the seminal totalitarian democrat who thought that man must "be forced to be free" because liberty "tacitly includes the undertaking, which alone can give force to [the social compact], that whoever refuses to obey the general will shall be compelled to do so by the whole body" of society.

How fitting, then that Justice Ginsburg chose Cairo, ground-zero of the "Arab Spring," as the setting for her speech. Even as she uttered words to consign America's fundamental law to the ash heap, Egypt's triumphant

Islamic supremacists were in the process of winning 80 percent of the seats in the new parliament. Their first major task will be the drafting of a new constitution—which is why Justice Ginsburg was asked to ruminate about America's in the first place. Only one thing is certain about the constitution the Muslim Brotherhood and its Islamist coalition partners will establish: Section Two of the current constitution, which makes Islam's repressive sharia supreme, will remain sacrosanct and be given real teeth. Ginsburg thinks our two-hundred-and-thirty-years-old Constitution is outdated, but at fourteen-hundred years old and counting, Islam's totalitarian legal code is practically primeval—and yet, here it is born anew. After all, it serves precisely the function that law serves in totalitarian democracy: It suppresses free expression, free will, and volition. Conformity eventually becomes "free choice" because it is the only available alternative. As Talmon put it, addressing the tension between freedom and the progressive vision:

> This difficulty could only be resolved by thinking not in terms of men as they are, but as they were meant to be, and would be, given the proper conditions. In so far as they are at variance with the absolute ideal they can be ignored, coerced or intimidated into conforming without any real violation of the democratic principle being involved. In the proper conditions, it is held, the conflict between spontaneity and duty would disappear, and with it the need for coercion. The practical question is, of course, whether constraint will disappear because all have learned to act in harmony, or because all opponents have been eliminated.

Islam, we are tirelessly reminded by its apologists citing Sura 2:256, prohibits compulsion in matters of religion. We need, however, to read the sharia fine-print. True,

Islam will not force you to become a believer—at least not officially. It has no compunction, however, about imposing what Talmon would call "the proper conditions"—the sharia system, which, in fact, assumes the presence in the caliphate of non-believers, whose subjugation has a sobering *in terrorem* effect (and whose obligatory poll tax promotes the sharia state's fiscal health). The concept is that with enough coercion, there will eventually be no need for coercion: everyone, of his own accord, will come to the good sense of becoming a Muslim—all other alternatives having been dhimmified into desuetude.

Post–World War II, "all the constitution writing" so admired by Justice Ginsburg for its promotion of human rights has become totalitarian democracy's cognate version of social engineering. It seeks to create the proper conditions that might mold us into what progressives think we are meant to be. The wellspring of this rights revolution is "international humanitarian law," a now bulging corpus of *bien pensant* pieties.

The global human rights movement represents over half a century's erosion of first principles: that nations are sovereign; that international standards may not be applied to them absent their consent; and that treaties are political agreements between national governments, not banquets of individual and largely redistributive "rights" that citizens may enforce judicially against national governments. This regression, from the venerable "Law of Nations" enshrined in our Constitution to today's amorphous international humanitarian law mirrors the ongoing contortion of domestic "rights" from freedom-preserving safeguards enjoyed by all citizens against government into freedom-killing intrusions into private life by government for the benefit of some citizens over others.

The "Law of Nations," derived from antiquity's *jus gentium* principle, was invoked by ancient Rome when the *jus civile,* the law applied to citizens, was inapposite. A bow to natural law, the principle recognized that basic strictures honored by diverse peoples across the empire must be grounded in human reason. This was the framers' classic meaning in empowering Congress to proscribe offenses against the Law of Nations. As construed by the English jurist William Blackstone, the grant was exceedingly narrow, relating only to piracy and the protection of diplomats.

Two centuries later, however, seizing on the previously moribund Alien Torts Act enacted in 1789 by the first Congress, the federal courts began expanding the doctrine to meddle in the affairs of other countries—for example, entertaining a lawsuit by Paraguayan victims tortured by Paraguayan officials in Paraguay. Today's judges rationalize that conduct should be actionable if, in their estimation, it transgresses "definable, universal, and obligatory norms." As night follows day, the busybody jurists of other nations reciprocate, claiming "universal jurisdiction" to hound former American government officials with "war crimes" investigations over their execution of U.S. policy.

The Law of Nations is not to be confused (which is to say, it is forever confused) with "international law." As George Mason University's Jeremy Rabkin explains, the latter is a broader concept, based on the mutuality of obligations between *consenting* sovereigns: "a law that was entirely *between* nations, rather than reaching into their internal affairs." The simplest iteration is the written treaty.

The Constitution makes treaties the supreme law of the land, provided they follow a fairly arduous ratification procedure: presidential agreement approved by two-thirds of the Senate. But nothing about the "rule of law" is ever simple for long. Once ratified, a treaty has the same legal force as a statute—or does it? In theory, a statute cannot override the Constitution, but in an obscure 1920 case, the Supreme Court held that, by striking down a treaty with Great Britain that regulated the hunting of migratory birds, the federal government effectively preempted the laws of Missouri—something that federalism and the separation-of-powers principle barred Congress from doing, bird hunting having always been a matter of sovereign state control. So, could Leviathan, by making a treaty with, say, Mexico, degrade or eviscerate other powers our allegedly outdated Constitution reserves to the states or the people? What does one suppose Justice Ginsburg would say?

The question is not idle. Treaty writing has exploded since World War II. Reeling from the unprecedented carnage, victorious nations undertook to prohibit war, or at least regulate it out of existence, convincing themselves that human nature could be altered by parchment. This was an irony coming from the generation that had endured a hellacious war precisely because it realized there were worse evils, like Fascism—a generation that watched Nazi atrocities give way to Soviet tyranny. Beyond the Geneva Conventions, the post-war era gave birth to the nascent United Nations' 1948 Universal Declaration of Human Rights.

To this day, the Declaration animates the rights revolution Justice Ginsburg now heralds. Midwifed by Eleanor Roosevelt, it proclaimed us all as a single "human family," collectively responsible to guarantee each other not just life, liberty, and property but personal security, freedom from torture, slavery, and arbitrary arrest, equality before the law, travel and asylum, employment with "just and favourable compensation," education, healthcare, food, clothing, housing, leisure time, and on and on. Today, the utopian world envisioned by the Declaration lives on in the economically sclerotic and unsustainable nations of continental Europe.

For all its dreamy rhetoric, the Declaration is merely hortatory, a tocsin, not a treaty. Moreover, the cold, hard fact that we are so *not* one big happy human family inevitably arrived in the form of an aggrieved Muslim response: the 1990 Declaration of Human Rights in Islam, which advocates the global hegemony of sharia. Nevertheless, numerous treaties were weaved from the original Declaration's nostrums. The two most prominent, by way of the United Nations, are the International Covenant on Civil and Political Rights and the International Covenant on Economic, Social and Cultural Rights. The former hopes to forbid degrading treatment, hate speech, advocacy of war, unequal burdens in child-rearing, and capital punishment (a later add-on). The latter is a progressive wish-list that envisions government-controlled economic sectors, comparative worth compensation, a mandate to end hunger, and universal healthcare (perhaps galactic healthcare was too modest). The torrent of human rights treaties eventually added conventions prohibiting discrimination against women, racial discrimination, torture, and cruel, inhuman, and degrading treatment, as well as conventions promoting the rights of migrant workers, the "rights of the child," and so on.

For the most part, the authoritarian and redistributive components of these monstrosities would stand little chance of being enacted into domestic law by Congress. Knowing that, presidents—especially those of a Leftist orientation—often play a cynical game. They sign on to the document as a show of internationalist solidarity but do not press for its ratification to avoid political damage at home. Who, after all, wants to be labeled as an opponent of such treacle as "the rights of the child"? And yet, who in America wants to be accountable for seeking to nationalize education, grant children rights of action against their parents, and, according to the drafting committee, require the criminalization of all corporal punishment? Justice Ginsburg's patron, President Bill Clinton, not only signed, but helped draft this convention. With even Somalia on board, it has become a source of no small embarrassment to President Obama that the United States is the only country on earth (besides the newly minted South Sudan) to refuse its ratification.

Alternatively, some human rights treaties do finally get ratified, but only after the Senate lards them with sweeping reservations and caveats. The UN Convention Against Torture is an example: while a government with weighty security responsibilities does not want to be seen as pro-torture, neither can it afford to endorse such inscrutably vague terms as a prohibition on "degrading treatment" (many Muslim men, for instance, find it degrading to be interrogated by a female investigator). So the UNCAT was ratified with the proviso that, other than torture—which is controlled by a federal statute—the "cruel, inhuman and degrading" terms do not proscribe anything not already forbidden by the Constitution.

The palpable objective of these precautions is to enable practical politicians to nullify lunatic treaties while ostensibly endorsing both the ideal of "human rights" and the illusion of an "international community"—each immensely popular among progressive academics and their media echo-chamber. The Constitution was once our insurance against the consequences of these shenanigans: absent clear, unconditional ratification, we could not be saddled with bad treaty terms even if presidents made a show of embracing them. This is no longer the case, though. The transnational Left, spearheaded by judges, law professors, bar associations, NGOs, and international bureaucrats, has devised several stratagems for defeating the Constitution's preference for American self-determination over foreign consensus.

The simplest of these devices is the "executive agreement," a favorite of presidents across the ideological divide. To avoid ratification disputes, presidents make deals with their counterparts in other nations, maintaining that their plenary authority over foreign affairs permits this autocratic streamlining. It also, they insist, dictates compliance at home, even if that means riding roughshod over both the constitutional check of Congress and the constitutional prerogatives of states and citizens. There is today no shortage of politicians, even self-avowed "conservatives," who urge that national security, or at least national honor, requires rallying behind the commander-in-chief, regardless of the fall-out.

Still, executive agreements can at least be seen, grasped, and theoretically undone by straightforward legislation. Far more troublesome is "customary" international law, which is not easily grasped because it is forever evolving and forever breaking with its own bedrock tenet of sovereign consent. This species of law is referred to as "custom" because there is no express agreement; abstract principles are simply deemed to have transmogrified into binding law once they achieve some mystical degree of claimed consensus. Deemed by whom, and based on what consensus? These are the questions, but the answers are elusive. What is "customary" turns out to be very much in the eye of the beholder—invariably, a progressive party, organization, or court desirous of radiating its statist predilections with the majesty of "law."

This is not to pooh-pooh the whole idea of custom. That some deeply rooted customs achieve nigh-global consensus is beyond a doubt. Were it not patently imperative that a nation's emissaries be given safe conduct in foreign lands and were pirates on the high seas not regarded as *hostis humani generis* (the enemy of humanity), there would be no foreign commerce to speak of— hence, the Law of Nations recognized by the framers. To take another example, the "laws and customs of war" were developed over centuries of international practice— limiting legitimate combat to sovereign states; proscribing intentional or disproportionate attacks against civilians; and requiring soldiers to identify themselves as such (wearing uniforms, carrying their arms openly, etc.).

Back when international understandings were not typically memorialized on paper, these truly were time-honored norms, basic and civilizing. It is unsurprising, then, that even after the modern spate of multilateral treaties commenced in the nineteenth century, it became, well, customary to insert the so-called "Martens Clause" (from the Hague Convention of 1899), stipulating that, notwithstanding the reduction of extensive agreements to writing, "populations and belligerents remain under the protection and empire of the principles of international law, as they result from the usages established between civilized nations, from the laws of humanity, and the requirements of the public conscience."

But that was before the ascendancy of the Lawyer Left. Once the rights revolution took hold, terms like the "laws of humanity" and the "public conscience" gave cavernous maneuvering room to progressives who see law as their social-justice cudgel. They play the "customary law" game

152

as follows: Some law is written and some is unspoken but widely accepted. As we've seen, countries may decline to adopt the written law by refusing to join treaties, signing but declining to ratify them, or freighting ratification with caveats, as the United States is wont to do when treaty terms against, say, free expression, gun ownership, or the death penalty run afoul of the Constitution. Yet, once a written treaty is adopted by a critical mass of countries over a period of years, progressives contend that it has been subsumed into customary law. This, they assert, means that even countries that have never consented are now obliged to submit to the treaty terms, as originally written by the international community's left-leaning lawyers, not as qualified by ratification caveats.

Thus, for example, does the Supreme Court circumvent the Constitution's treaty-ratification procedure by citing unratified treaties. In 2010, for example, Justice Anthony Kennedy cited the Convention on the Rights of the Child in invalidating a Florida law that permitted a minor to be sentenced to life imprisonment for a non-homicide offense. Justice Kennedy is the centrist "swing justice" who, like Justice Ginsburg and the Court's three other reliable Leftists, trends transnational-progressive in human rights cases. He rationalized that the Eighth Amendment bar against cruel and unusual punishment had expanded to include the provisions of the unratified treaty and other indicia of global decency norms— "global" and "norms" evidently excluding the law and practices actually followed in land masses east, west, and south of the Euro Zone sliver.

Worse, in elevating their sensibilities over democratic self-determination, customary law enthusiasts do not limit themselves to treaty terms that have never been ratified. Rather, as Adam Roberts and Richard Guelff detail in their essential treatise, *Documents on the Laws of War*, customary law is also informed by, among other things: (a) diplomatic, political, and military behavior by states (including their official statements, court decisions, legislation, and administrative decrees); (b) the judicial decisions of international tribunals such as the United Nations International Court of Justice (the pretentiously self-styled "World Court" which, for example, ruled in 2004 that Israel's security fence, a passive security measure that reduced Palestinian suicide bombing attacks by over 90 percent, somehow violated international law); (c) the International Criminal Court (which claims jurisdiction over the United States despite our refusal to join); (d) such *ad hoc* tribunals as those established at Nuremburg and Tokyo after World War II, and after the genocides in Rwanda and Yugoslavia in the mid–1990s; (e) treatises and other writings by international law experts interpreting treaties and customs; (f) military manuals; (g) the proceedings of the United Nations and its various components (which tend to be rabidly anti-Israeli and anti-American); and (h) interpretive publications and conventions produced by such influential (and reliably progressive) non-governmental organizations as the International Committee of the Red Cross, Amnesty International, and Human Rights Watch.

On the international stage, human rights revolutionaries do not content themselves with inventing law out of thin air and the minutes of progressive gab-fests. They have perverted the very idea of the treaty, and thus of the point of having international law at all.

Since 1648, when the Treaty of Westphalia for the most part ended a century of war in Europe, the sovereign nation-state has been the foundation of the international order. Law is essentially a domestic affair. Treaties are political agreements between sovereigns, and violations of them are the stuff of diplomacy, which can run the gamut from compromise to appeasement to economic sanctions to war. Judicial processes may not be imposed on sovereigns without their consent, either in the courts of another nation or in international tribunals.

The human rights revolution seeks to cataclysmically change these assumptions. Transnational progressives are post-sovereign. They see nation-states like they see the U.S. Constitution: as obsolete. Theirs is not a world—like the real one—in which order is kept by the assurance that sovereigns will pursue their interests and use force as necessary to maintain security. It is a mirage: a global legal order overseen by supranational agencies and managed by courts, whose writs will be enforced by—er, well, never mind. Enforcement will be unnecessary in a world devoted to the rule of law, meaning all that old-fashioned military spending can be diverted to healthcare, retirement security, education, housing, employment, and recreation.

In such a world, treaties are not sovereign-to-sovereign agreements. They are repositories of rights that run to the individual, who may enforce them in court. That the treaties would never have been entertained in the first place if that were the case—that there would be no Geneva Conventions had Harry Truman, Dwight Eisenhower, and the post-war Senate understood that al Qaeda could one day use them to put the United States on trial in our own courts over the manner in which we wage a war that the terrorists started—is beside the point for progressives. Professor Rabkin observes that this is a radical departure: until recently, "talk of an 'international law of human rights' would have seemed . . . oxymoronic." International law used to mean that sovereigns would protest the mistreatment of their own citizens in foreign territory. But the central conceit of "human rights law"—namely, that a growing body of rights and privileges "apply to human beings, as such" and may be judicially enforced by them, even against their own governments, even if their fellow citizens have not consented—would have been thought absurd.

So what is the end game? When acolytes of totalitarian democracy gush, as Justice Ginsburg did, over the foreign embrace of "basic human rights," they are celebrating a radical transformation not just of international law but also of what a "right" is.

In 2001, Illinois State Senator Barack Obama gave an interview to Chicago Public Radio in which he lamented the timorousness of the Warren Court. Now, most Americans remember the Supremes of the Sixties and Seventies as a rather revolutionary bunch—blazing the trail on abortion, the rights of the criminal, and today's imperial judiciary. To Obama, though, they had flinched. They had failed to confront "the issues of redistribution of wealth, and of more basic issues such as political and economic justice in society."

It was an early glimpse of the change agent who, as a presidential candidate seven years later, would admonish an ordinary Ohioan named Joe Wurzelbacher, now known to America as "Joe the Plumber," that social progress could come only when government "spread the wealth around." The Warren Court, Obama explained back in 2001, failed to "break free from the essential constraints that were placed by the founding fathers in the Constitution." Instead, Obama complained, the justices clung to the hoary construction of the Constitution as "a charter of negative liberties," one that says only what government "can't do to you." Obama explained that real economic justice demands the *positive* case: what government "must do on your behalf."

This philosophy is a reprise of what Jonah Goldberg elegantly calls the "apotheosis of liberal aspirations." It first surfaced in President Franklin D. Roosevelt's 1944 proposal of a "Second Bill of Rights," a mandate that government construct "a new basis of security and prosperity." The new guarantees—which, not coincidentally, also found their way into Mrs. Roosevelt's Universal Declaration of Human Rights—would include "a useful and remunerative job," "a decent home," "adequate medical care and the opportunity to achieve and enjoy good health," "adequate protection from the economic fears of old age, sickness, accident, and unemployment," and a "good education."

This is the dream of totalitarian democracy, and Obama hopes to be its political Messiah. Law is to be the principal tool for achieving it. Politically, it cannot be done: the cost would be too prohibitive even if a rising tide of citizens were not already growing restive over the debt crisis that Washington blithely ignores. Thus, the Left's reliance on law: Americans like to see themselves as law-abiding—which is why politicians lace their rhetoric with allusions to the "rule of law" though they exhibit scant allegiance to the law in their own machinations. Americans are apt to abide even that which they deeply resent if they come to believe the law requires it.

The sad irony is that the inversion of rights from safeguards to entitlements is a profound betrayal of our fundamental law. The political commentator Mark Levin has explained it well:

> This is tyranny's disguise. These are not rights. They are the Statist's false promises of utopianism, which the Statist uses

to justify all trespasses on the individual's private property. Liberty and private property go hand in hand. By dominating one, the Statist dominates both, for if the individual cannot keep or dispose of the value he creates by his own intellectual and/or physical labor, he exists to serve the state. The "Second Bill of Rights" and its legal and policy progeny require the individual to surrender control of his fate to the government.

For the framers, government was a necessary evil. It was required for a free people's collective security but, if insufficiently checked, it was guaranteed to devour liberty. The purpose of the Constitution was not to make the positive case for *government*. The case for government is the case for submission—submission to, as Talmon put it, the "sole and exclusive truth," the progressives' "absolute collective purpose," their "proper conditions" for making men not what they are but what "they were meant to be."

In stark contrast, the Constitution is the positive case for *freedom*—real freedom, not freedom in the sense (actually, the nonsense) of Rousseau, the Islamists, and totalitarian democracy, in which the individual complies because a coercive environment leaves him with no other options. Freedom cannot exist without order, and thus implies some measure of government. It is, however, a limited government, vested with only the powers expressly enumerated in the law of the land, our Constitution. As the framers knew, a government that strays beyond those powers is necessarily treading on freedom's territory. It is certain to erode the very "Blessings of Liberty" the Constitution was designed to secure. Freedom is our protection from that kind of government.

There is a positive argument to be made for government, and the Constitution does not ignore it. It is eloquently stated in the document's opening lines, which enjoin government to establish justice and protect national security. These injunctions are vital: there is no liberty without them. But they do not involve social engineering or the picking of winners and losers. These guarantees, instead, are for *everyone,* uniformly: Government must "provide for the *common* defense" and "promote the *general* welfare." The Blessings of Liberty are to be secured "to ourselves and to our posterity"—not to yourself at the expense of my posterity.

We are in an age of upheaval, and what becomes of our law will go a long way toward determining how it ends. In a free society such as ours, grounded in a culture of ordered liberty, law should not be a didactic force. It undergirds economic and social life as it is already lived, reflecting the society's values rather than instructing the society on what to think and how to live. But today's progressive legal elites would have it another way. To them, the "rule of law" is code for a "social justice" crusade in which the courts, government bureaucracies, and international tribunals replace democratic self-determination with their sole and exclusive truth. If the progressives get their way, upheaval will not yield utopia. It will yield totalitarianism.

Out of the Wilderness

Charles Murray

UPON READING Daniel Boorstin's *The Discoverers* many years ago, I became fascinated with the ebbs and flows of human achievement, and especially those points in world history that have been associated with a flowering of great accomplishment. The most famous are Athens in the Periclean age and Florence in the Renaissance, but there have been many other less spectacular examples. Sometimes, the surge of great creativity is most obvious in a particular domain—literature in nineteenth-century Russia, for example—but strides made in one field are usually accompanied by strides made in others. Historically speaking, what accounts for the difference in the fertility of the cultural ground?

In the late 1990s, I set out to assemble data-bases of humanity's great achievements, applying historiometric methods to identify the significant figures and remarkable achievements. The result was a book I published in 2004, *Human Accomplishment: The Pursuit of Excellence in the Arts and Sciences, 800 B.C. to 1950.* In its concluding chapters, I laid out the conditions (italicized in the rest of this essay) that characterize the times and places in which accomplishment has flourished. The question I seek to answer in this essay is: Given what we know about the conditions that led to great accomplishment in the past, what are the prospects for great accomplishment in the arts as we move through the twenty-first century? I begin with the conditions that are empirically indisputable and work my way to ones that are more interpretive.

A major stream of human accomplishment is facilitated by growing national wealth, both through the additional money that can support the arts and sciences and through the indirect spillover effects of economic growth on cultural vitality.

National wealth is an enabling condition. It doesn't ensure great accomplishment, but it provides the where-withal for patrons to buy works of art and boxes at the concert hall. Economic growth is also a signal of a civilization's vitality and confidence, which is likely to be mirrored in the vitality and creativity of its arts. In this regard, the news is good for the United States. We are very rich and we are likely to continue to get richer, assuming current economic policies don't continue forever. The United States is unlikely to be impeded from great accomplishment by a lack of wealth.

A major stream of human accomplishment is fostered by the existence of cities that serve as centers of human capital and supply audiences and patrons for the arts.

America has several urban centers that provide the critical mass of human capital necessary for great accomplishment.

A major stream of human accomplishment is fostered by political regimes that give de facto freedom of action to their potential artists and scholars.

No problem here either, though it should be noted that the requirements for political freedom are not stringent. Some of the great streams of accomplishment have occurred under absolute monarchies—Louis XIV's France comes to mind—when the monarch allowed artists to work unmolested. In contemporary America, scientific research in both the hard and soft sciences is constrained on some topics by political correctness and even government restrictions (e.g., stem cell research). But composers, painters, sculptors, and authors still have plenty of freedom of action.

A major stream of human accomplishment is fostered by a culture that encourages the belief that individuals can act efficaciously as individuals, and encourages them to do so.

The creative act in painting, sculpture, musical composition, or writing comes down to a solitary person thinking of something new and pursuing it without knowing for sure what the result will be. Any culture will turn out some audacious, self-willed people in that vein. But the more collectivist, communitarian, or familial a culture is, the fewer such individuals will emerge, and the greater the damping effect on artistic creation will be. Thus, classical China was a highly familial society with stunning achievements in painting and poetry, but there was much less innovation and branching out in those artistic fields than in the West. When Confucianism was the reigning philosophical paradigm, the aesthetic rules set down by revered poets and painters could remain nearly intact for centuries.

Once again, it is hard to find reasons for thinking that America has a problem meeting this criterion. We continue to be a highly individualistic culture. If anything, our most talented have too inflated a sense of their ability to act efficaciously as individuals.

The best single predictor of a stream of accomplishment in the current generation is the presence of great models in the previous generation.

The insight that great accomplishment begets more great accomplishment goes back two thousand years to a

Roman, Velleius Paterculus, who first analyzed the clustering of genius in Athens and concluded that "genius is fostered by emulation." In the modern era, that insight has been confirmed in rigorous quantitative studies, and it is one of those social science findings that shouldn't surprise anyone. If children who have the potential for creating great art are watching a Leonardo da Vinci set the standard, they are more likely to create art like Michelangelo, Dürer, or Raphael did. This is relevant for thinking about the future of American accomplishment in the arts because, as far as I can see, we do not have any great models in the current generation who will produce greatness in the next generation.

The magnitude and content of a stream of accomplishment in a given domain varies according to the richness and age of the organizing structure.

The problem here is that we are living at a time when the rich organizing structures that gave us five centuries of magnificent accomplishments in the visual arts, music, and literature from 1400–1900 are old and filled up.

By *organizing structure,* I mean the principles, tools, and craft used to generate the artistic product. As an example, consider the organizing structure of painting as it was revolutionized in the fifteenth century. The new set of principles were those of linear perspective; a major new tool was invented in the form of oil paints; and the techniques that were developed to take advantage of the new principles and tool constituted an elevated level of craft. Together, they formed an organizing structure for creating two-dimensional art that was incredibly rich with possibilities and unleashed a flood of great work. Music saw the development of an equally promising new organizing structure over a longer period, from the late middle ages through the Baroque period, with the creation of polyphony and eventually tonal harmony (principles), new and improved instruments (tools), and the evolution of techniques for taking advantage of the new resources (craft). In literature, the organizing structure that created an eruption of great work starting in the late eighteenth century was overwhelmingly dominated by a new principle: the modern novel.

All of these organizing structures are more than two centuries old. Even the systematic use of abstraction in the visual arts (a new set of principles) has been around for more than a century and a half. In other words, all of the organizing structures for the great artistic works of the West have been largely "filled up," in a practical sense. It is theoretically true, as Arnold Schoenberg famously said, that plenty of good music remains to be written in C major. But artists want to break new ground, and the more creative power an artist possesses, the less likely it is that he wants to produce another version of a well-established form. What's the point of writing a great symphony in the classical style (from the ambitious composer's point of view), when we already have so many of them?

This doesn't mean that a second renaissance is impossible within these ageing organizing structures, but it would have to be sparked by a renewed passion for the kind of art they permit—a renewed passion for the things that can be conveyed by the "window on the world" of realistic art, tonal harmony harnessed to grand themes, and fictional narratives stuffed full of life. Absent that fundamental change in the satisfactions artists take from their creations, we will need new organizing structures to give their potential full rein.

The richest new organizing structure of the twentieth century was the motion picture. It is also the only organizing structure that does not show signs of being filled up. A plausible case can be made that the film industry is still making products that rank somewhere among the all-time best, and there is reason to hope that even better are yet to come.

What are the prospects for the discovery of completely new organizing structures in the arts? It's hard to tell. Until a new organizing structure appears, how can one identify the void that it fills? But I will cautiously advance the possibility that we are approaching limits dictated by human evolution.

Consider the dead-end organizing structure that appeared during the twentieth century: the atonality (or contra-tonality) that Arnold Schoenberg thought would rival tonal harmony for the public's affection. He was wrong. Neuroscientists are identifying the reasons why he was wrong. Music based on tonal harmony is attractive for reasons that go deep into the brain, and atonality creates an instinctive aversion in most persons for equally deep reasons. In his book *The Art Instinct,* Denis Dutton has a fascinating account of the characteristics of landscape paintings that appeal to humans across cultures and across time, and persuasively links those characteristics to human responses that were hard-wired in the early phases of human evolution. Human traditions of storytelling suggest that humans are hard-wired to prefer certain narrative conventions.

Still, humans are adaptable. Some of Mozart's and Beethoven's music was considered painfully dissonant when it was first played, and much of Stravinsky's work has become a lasting part of the repertoire. Expressionism left "window on the world" realism behind, but humans still responded enthusiastically to the expressionists' new conventions for capturing reality. Innovations in novelistic narrative using stream of consciousness have gained acceptance.

But humans are adaptable only up to a point. True, some people say they love Arnold Schoenberg's music, respond in some important way to Andy Warhol's art, and have read *Gravity's Rainbow* all the way through. But they constitute a small minority. Most people are drawn to tonal music, pictorial art, and literature that is centered on storytelling for reasons that go back to the ancient African savanna.

If that proposition is correct, then the prospects for the emergence of important new organizing structures are limited when it comes to content that appeals to a wide audience. Instead, they must depend on possibilities created by new technology. In music, wonderful new instruments could enable new varieties of music that tap into the same inborn needs that C major satisfies. Technology might give visual artists new ways of creating works that appeal to the same instincts that have the made pictorial art so beloved. Electronic video games may evolve into a new organizing structure for storytelling that eventually will produce great cultural products. And who knows what symbiosis between humans and technology will eventually be developed, enabling artists and their technological muses to create jointly works that rise above the bar set by the great masters of the past? At least we can always hope.

A major stream of human accomplishment is fostered by a culture in which the most talented people believe that life has a purpose and that the function of life is to fulfill that purpose.

Imagine two cultures with exactly equal numbers of potentially brilliant artists. One is a culture in which those potentially brilliant artists have a strong sense of "this is what I was put on this earth to do," and in the other, nihilism reigns. In both cultures, the potentially brilliant artists can come to enjoy the exercise of their capabilities. But the nihilists are at a disadvantage in two respects.

The first disadvantage is in the motivation to take on the intense and unremitting effort that is typically required to do great things. This is one of the most overlooked aspects of great accomplishment. Fame can come easily and overnight, but excellence is almost always accompanied by a crushing workload. Psychologists have put specific dimensions to this aspect of accomplishment. One thread of this literature, inaugurated in the early 1970s by Herbert Simon, argues that expertise in a subject requires a person to assimilate about 50,000 "chunks" of information about the subject over about ten years of experience—simple expertise, not the mastery that is associated with great accomplishment. Once expertise is achieved, it is followed by thousands of hours of practice, study, and labor.

The willingness to engage in such monomaniacal levels of effort in the arts is related to a sense of vocation. By vocation, I have in mind the dictionary definition of "a function or station in life to which one is called by God." God needn't be the source. Many achievers see themselves as having a vocation without thinking about where it came from. My point is that the characteristics of nihilism—ennui, anomie, alienation, and other forms of belief that life is futile and purposeless—are at odds with the zest and life-affirming energy needed to produce great art.

The second disadvantage involves the artist's choice of content. If life is purposeless, no one kind of project is intrinsically more important than any other kind. Take, for example, an extraordinarily talented screenwriter who is an atheist and a cynic. When asked if he has a purpose in life, he says, "Sure, to make as much money as I can," and he means it. The choice of content in his screenplays is driven by their commercial potential. His screenplays are brilliantly written, but it is a coincidence if they deal with great themes of the human condition. His treatment of those great themes, even when he happens to touch on them, is not driven by a passion to illuminate, but to exploit. If instead he has a strong sense of "This is what I was put on earth to do," the choice of content will matter, because he has a strong sense that what he does is meaningful. To believe life has a purpose carries with it a predisposition to put one's talents in the service of the highest expression of one's vocation.

Thinking ahead to the rest of the twenty-first century, the problem is that the artistic elites have been conspicuously nihilist for the last century, and the rest of the culture has recently been following along. The most direct cause of a belief that one's life has a purpose—belief in a personal God who wants you to use your gifts to the fullest—has been declining rapidly throughout society, and the plunge has steepened since the early 1990s. The rejection of traditional religion is especially conspicuous among intellectual and artistic elites.

A major stream of accomplishment in any domain requires a well-articulated vision of, and use of, the transcendental goods relevant to that domain.

In the classic Western tradition, the worth of something that exists in our world can be characterized by its embodiment of truth, beauty, or the good. Truth and beauty are familiar concepts, but "the good" is not a term in common use these days, so I should spell out that I am using it in the sense that Aristotle did in the opening sentence of the *Nicomachean Ethics*: "Every art and every inquiry, and similarly every action and pursuit, is thought to aim at some good; and for this reason the good has rightly been declared to be that at which all things aim." When applied to human beings, the essence of "the good" is not a set of ethical rules that one struggles to follow, but a vision of human flourishing that attracts and draws one onward.

The proposition I argued in *Human Accomplishment* is that great accomplishment in the arts is anchored in one or more of these three transcendental goods. The arts can rise to the highest rungs of craft without them, but, in the same way that a goldsmith needs gold, a culture that fosters great accomplishment needs a coherent sense of transcendental goods. "Coherent sense" means that the goods are a live presence in the culture, and that great artists compete to approach them. This doesn't mean that in, say, Renaissance Italy, every artist spent his days thinking about what beauty meant, but that a coherent conception of "beauty" was in the air, and it was taken for granted that art drew from that understanding.

Beauty is not the only transcendental good that the arts require. A coherent sense of the good is also important—perhaps not so much for great music (though I may be wrong about that), but often for great art and almost always for great literature. I do not mean that a great painting has to be beautiful in a saccharine sense or that great novels must be moral fables that could qualify for *McGuffey's Readers*. Rather, a painter's or a novelist's conception of the meaning of a human life provides the frame within which the artist translates the varieties of human experience into art. The artistic treatment of violence offers an example. In the absence of a conception of the good, the depiction of violence is sensationalism at best—think Sam Peckinpah. When the depiction of violence is taken to extremes, it can have the same soul-corroding effect as pornography. But when it is informed by a conception of the good, the depiction of violence can have great artistic power—think *Macbeth*. So whereas some great works of art, music, and even literature are not informed by a conception of the good, the translation of this concept to the canvas or the written word is often what separates enduring art from entertainment. Extract its moral vision, and Goya's *The Third of May 1808* becomes a violent cartoon. Extract its moral vision, and *Huckleberry Finn* becomes *Tom Sawyer*.

To generalize my argument regarding the importance of the transcendental goods, I believe that when artists do not have coherent ideals of beauty, their work tends to be sterile; when they do not have coherent ideals of the good, their work tends to be vulgar. Without either beauty or the good, their work tends to be shallow. Artistic accomplishment that is sterile, vulgar, and shallow does not endure.

These observations are especially relevant to our era because in the twentieth century, truth, beauty, and the good were outright rejected in the culture. I am referring to the rise of certain nihilistic strains in modernism, which took root in the last half of the nineteenth century, broke into bloom in the years just before World War I, and reached full flower in the 1920s and 1930s. In *From Dawn to Decadence,* Jacques Barzun described the three strategies used by the avant-garde to advance its agenda:

> One, to take the past and present and make fun of everything in it by parody, pastiche, ridicule, and desecration, to signify rejection. Two, return to the bare elements of the art and, excluding ideas and ulterior purpose, play variations on those elements simply to show their sensuous power and the pleasure afforded by bare technique. Three, remain serious but find ways to get rid of the past by destroying the very idea of art itself.

Sometimes, the new way of thinking was expressed cynically. "To be able to think freely," André Gide wrote, "one must be certain that what one writes will be of no consequence." Sometimes the proponents of the new art used the language of the transcendental goods with an Orwellian redefinition, as in Guillaume Apollinaire's pronouncement that the modern school of painting "wants to visualize beauty disengaged from whatever charm man has for man." By the mid-twentieth century, the abstract painter Barnett Newman put it more brutally: He and his colleagues were acting out of "the desire to destroy beauty."

Postmodernism has followed modernism. In the visual arts, the repudiation of the transcendental goods was taken to new extremes. Some of the specific sensations, such as Mapplethorpe's sadomasochistic photographs and Serrano's *Piss Christ*, have become nationally famous. In some schools of contemporary music, the aspect of truth that is so compelling in Bach—the mathematical inevitability of some of his music—has been transmuted into extremely intricate mathematical puzzles, but puzzles that are devoid of beauty or emotion. In literature, modern novelists linger on the anxieties of the human condition, but seldom draw on a conception of the good as a resource for illuminating that condition.

I take these potshots at modernism and postmodernism aware that exceptions exist. I also happily report that the postmodernists are feeling some pushback. In *The Blank Slate,* Steven Pinker listed some of the movements—the Derriere Guard, Radical Center, Natural Classicism, the New Formalism, the New Narrativism, Stuckism, the Return of Beauty, and No Mo Po Mo— that are trying to fuse innovation in the arts with coherent conceptions of what I call the transcendental goods.

Wendy Steiner's *Venus in Exile* is a damning indictment of the postmodernists' rejection of beauty, but she is able to point to many examples of the return of coherent conceptions of beauty in recent years. With those caveats, this generalization about the early twenty-first century still seems justified: The postmodern sensibility still dominates the current generation of visual artists, composers, literary critics, and "serious" novelists, and, to that extent, the renunciation of the transcendental goods remains.

Drawing these strands together, my analysis of the patterns of past streams of accomplishment leads to a mixed prognosis for the future. America, as it enters the second decade of the twenty-first century, has the physical infrastructure for great achievement in the arts: national wealth and vibrant urban centers. Its potential artists have sufficient freedom of action. The American culture still fosters a sense of personal autonomy and efficaciousness.

But it does not have a generation of great models for the next generation to emulate. The organizing structures that produced the oeuvres of great past accomplishment in literature, painting, sculpture, and music are old and filled up. Even the newest organizing structure, surrounding motion pictures, is a hundred years old at this point. The twentieth century saw a steep decline in religious faith among the elite, which presumably is associated with a steep decline in the sense of the "this-is-what-I-was-put-on-earth-to-do" motivation to create great work. The same century saw a rejection of the transcendental goods that I believe are part of the indispensable raw material for great achievement in the arts.

So we have the infrastructure for a major stream of accomplishment, but not the culture for one. On top of that major obstacle are three other potential problems that I must put as questions because my analysis of

CHARLES MURRAY

previous human history can give us no direct answers to them. Can a major stream of artistic accomplishment be produced by a society that is geriatric? By a society that is secular? By an advanced welfare state?

History gives us no direct answers because we are facing unprecedented situations. We have never observed a great civilization with a population as old as the United States will have in the twenty-first century; we have never observed a great civilization that is as secular as we are apparently going to become; and we have had only half a century of experience with advanced welfare states. But we need to think about these questions. The aging of the population is a demographic certainty. The prudent expectation, based on trends over the last fifty years, is that by mid-century the United States will be about as secular as Western and Northern Europe are now, and that the United States will have a welfare state indistinguishable from those of Western and Northern Europe. Neither of the latter two events is as inevitable as the aging of our society, but an alternative future would require a sharp U-turn in existing trends. What happens to the arts if these things come to pass?

The aging of society is about to accelerate, and the effects will probably be nonlinear. In 1900, only 13 percent of the population was over fifty years of age. By 1950, the proportion had grown to 23 percent. By 2000, not a lot had changed, with 27 percent of the population over fifty. But by 2050, current projections show the United States with 40 percent of its population over fifty, and that number could rise even higher with the advances in prolonging life that scientific advances are opening up. By 2100, the over-fifties will presumably constitute well over half of the population.

174

We cannot know for certain how the aging of the population will play out culturally, but it is hard to think of scenarios in which the arts become more vibrant and creative. It is possible that an aging population will facilitate a renewal of interest in the transcendental goods—people generally get more concerned about the great issues of life as they get older. But one of the constants of human history is that the creation of great art is dominated by the young—the median age of peak accomplishment is forty—and the milieu in which great art is created is surely facilitated by energy, freshness of outlook, optimism, and a sense of open-ended possibilities. We must assume that all of these will be in shorter supply than in the past now that our society is increasingly populated by the old.

The aging of the population is happening not only because of low birth rates, but also because life expectancy is increasing, which leads to another phenomenon without historic precedent: the removal of the constant psychological awareness that one's own death could happen at any time. The early death of a close friend or family member happens so rarely in the lives of most people that it has become an anomaly—today, we see the deaths of people in their sixties described as "untimely." Our baseline assumption is that we're going to live to old age. How is this affecting the human drive to achieve?

In a world where people of all ages die often and unexpectedly, there's a palpable urgency to getting on with whatever you're going to do with your life. If you don't leave your mark *now*, you may never get the chance. If you live in a world where you're sure you're going to live until at least eighty, do you have the same compulsion to leave your mark now? Or do you figure that there's still plenty of time left, and you'll get to it pretty soon? To what extent does enjoying life—since you can be sure there's going to be so much to enjoy—start to take precedence over maniacal efforts to leave a mark?

I raise the issue because it fits so neatly with the problems associated with increased secularism and the increased material security provided by the advanced welfare state. In a world when death can come at any time, there is also a clear and present motivation to think about spiritual matters even when you are young. Who knows when you're going to meet your Maker? It could easily be tomorrow. If you're going to live to be at least eighty, it's a lot easier not to think about the prospect of nonexistence. The world before the welfare state didn't give you the option of just passing the time pleasantly. Your main resources for living a comfortable life—or even for surviving at all—were hard work and family (especially, having children to support you in your old age). In the advanced welfare state, neither of those is necessary. The state will make sure you have a job, and one that doesn't require you to work too hard, and will support you in your old age.

Put all three conditions together—no urgency to make your mark, no promptings to think about your place in the cosmos, no difficulty in living a comfortable life—and what you seem to get, based on the experience of Western and Northern Europe, is what I have elsewhere called the Europe Syndrome.

The Europe Syndrome starts with a conception of humanity that is devoid of any element of the divine or even specialness. Humans are not intrinsically better or more important than other life forms, including trees. The Europe Syndrome sees human beings as collections of chemicals that are activated and, after a period of time, deactivated. The purpose of life is to while away the

°intervening time between birth and death as pleasantly as ossible. I submit that this way of looking at life is fundamentally incompatible with a stream of major accomplishment in the arts.

The most direct indictment of the Europe Syndrome as an incubator of great accomplishment in the arts is the European record since World War II. What are the productions of visual art, music, or literature that we can be confident will still be part of the culture two centuries from now, in the sense that hundreds of European works from two centuries ago are part of our culture today? We may argue over individual cases, and agree that the number of surviving works since World War II will be greater than zero, but it cannot be denied that the body of great work coming out of post-war Europe is pathetically thin compared to Europe's magnificent past.

The indirect indictment of the Europe Syndrome consists of the evidence that it is complicit in the loss of the confidence, vitality, and creative energy that provide a nourishing environment for great art. I blame primarily the advanced welfare state. Consider the ironies. The European welfare states brag about their lavish "child-friendly" policies, and yet they have seen plunging birth rates and marriage rates. They brag about their lavish protections of job security and benefits and yet, with just a few exceptions, their populations have seen falling proportions of people who find satisfaction in their work. They brag that they have eliminated the need for private charities, and their societies have become increasingly atomistic and anomic.

The advanced welfare state drains too much of the life from life. When there's no family, no community, no sense of vocation, and no faith, nothing is left except to pass away the time as pleasantly as possible.

I believe this self-absorption in whiling away life as pleasantly as possible explains why Europe has become a continent that no longer celebrates greatness. When I have spoken in Europe about the unparalleled explosion of European art and science from 1400 to 1900, the reaction of the audiences has invariably been embarrassment. Post-colonial guilt explains some of this reaction—Europeans seem obsessed with seeing the West as a force for evil in the world. But I suggest that another psychological dynamic is at work. When life has become a matter of passing away the time, being reminded of the greatness of your forebears is irritating and threatening.

Is there any way for the American arts to flourish even if we don't make a political U-turn and stave off the European welfare state? In trying to think about how a renaissance might happen, I cannot put aside the strongest conclusion that I took away from the work that went into *Human Accomplishment:* Religiosity is indispensable to a major stream of artistic accomplishment.

By "religiosity" I do not mean going to church every Sunday. Even belief in God is not essential. Confucianism, Daoism, and Buddhism are not religions in the conventional sense of that word—none postulates a God—but they partake of religiosity as I am using the word, in that that they articulate a human place in the cosmos, lay out understandings of the ends toward which human life aims, and set standards for seeking those ends.

A secular version of this framework exists, and forms a central strand in the Western tradition: the Aristotelian conception of human happiness and its intimate link with unceasing effort to realize the best that humans have within them. In practice, we know that the Aristotelian understanding of human flourishing works. A great many secular people working long hours and striving for perfection in all kinds of jobs are motivated by this view of human life, even if they don't realize it is Aristotelian.

Whether it happens in a theological or Aristotelian sense, I believe that religiosity has to suffuse American high culture once again if there is to be a renaissance of great art. Is that possible? And if it is, is it realistic? Thinking through such questions would take another essay at least as long as this one. But let me close by offering a reason for optimism.

The falling away from religiosity that we have seen over the last century must ultimately be anomalous. From the Enlightenment through Darwin, Freud, and Einstein, religiosity suffered a series of body blows. The verities understood in the old ways could not survive them. Not surprisingly, new expressions of those truths were not immediately forthcoming, and the West has been wandering in the wilderness.

It won't last forever. Humans are ineluctably drawn to fundamental questions of existence. "Why is there something rather than nothing?" is one such question. "What does it mean to live a good life?" is another. The elites who shape the milieu for America's high culture have managed to avoid thinking about those fundamental questions for a century now. Sooner or later, they'll find it too hard.

The Fourth Revolution

James Piereson

THE UNITED STATES has been shaped by three far-reaching political revolutions: Thomas Jefferson's "revolution of 1800," the Civil War, and the New Deal. Each of these upheavals concluded with lasting institutional and cultural adjustments that set the stage for new phases of political and economic development. Are we on the verge of a new upheaval, a "fourth revolution" that will reshape U.S. politics for decades to come? There are signs to suggest that we are. In fact, we may already be in the early stages of this twenty-first-century revolution.

The great recession that began in 2008 caused many to suggest that the United States is entering a period of "decline" during which it will lose its status as the world's most powerful and prosperous nation state. The metaphor of "decline" presumes that the American people will sit by passively as their standard of living and international status erode year by year. That is unlikely to occur: Americans will do everything in their power to reverse any such process of national decline. Thus, what the United States is now facing is not a gradual decline but a political upheaval that will reshape its politics, policies, and institutions for a generation or two to come. There is no guarantee that the nation will emerge from this crisis with its superpower status intact, just as there were no guarantees that it would emerge from the Civil War or the Great Depression in a position to extend its wealth and power. The most that we can say is that, in the decade ahead, Americans will struggle to forge a governing coalition that can guide the nation toward a path of renewed growth and dynamism.

The financial crisis and the long recession, with the strains they have placed upon national income and public budgets, are only the proximate causes of the political crisis now unfolding in the United States. The deeper causes lie in the exhaustion of the post-war system of political economy that took shape in the 1930s and 1940s. One pillar of that system emerged out of the New Deal with its emphasis upon national regulation of the economy, social insurance, expanding personal consumption, and public debt; the second emerged out of World War II with the U.S. dollar as the world's reserve currency and the U.S. military as the protector of the international trading system. The post-war system created the basis for unprecedented prosperity in the United States and the Western world. That system is now unwinding for several reasons, not least because the American economy can no longer underwrite the debt and public promises that have piled up over the decades. The urgent need to cancel or renegotiate these debts and public promises on short notice will ignite the upheaval referred to here as "the fourth revolution." There will follow an extended period of conflict in the United States between the two political parties as they compete for support either to maintain the post-war system or to identify a successor to it.

It is not possible to outline in advance the precise lineaments of the fourth revolution. After all, few Americans living in 1798, 1858, or 1928 could have foreseen what was going to happen to their country in the years immediately ahead. The best that we can do is to look for some general patterns in these earlier events that might serve as guides for what is likely to happen in the United States in the next decade or two.

Notwithstanding its reputation for stability and continuity, the U.S. political system seems to resolve its deepest problems in relatively brief periods of intense and potentially destabilizing conflict. These events are what some historians have called our "surrogates for revolution" because, rather than overthrowing the constitutional order, they adjust it to developing circumstances.

There are a few clear reasons why the American system adjusts in this discontinuous fashion. The constitutional system, with its dispersed powers and competing institutional interests, resists preemptive and over-arching solutions to accumulating problems. At the same time, America's dynamic economy and highly mobile society are constantly creating new challenges to which the political system cannot easily respond. At times, these challenges have built up to a point where the differences between parties and interests have been so fundamental as to defy efforts to resolve them through the ordinary channels of politics.

There are a few superficial similarities in the structure of these earlier events that might provide clues as to what we might look for in any new upheaval. These events—Jefferson's revolution, the sectional conflict, and the crisis of the 1930s and 1940s—extended over several election cycles before producing a stable resolution; the political settlements that emerged from these conflicts lasted roughly a lifetime—sixty or seventy years—until they began to unravel under the pressure of new developments; and each event ended with the ouster of the political party that had dominated the system during the previous era.

At a deeper level, each of these realignments discredited an established set of governing elites and brought into power new groups of political and cultural leaders. After reorganizing national politics around new principles, these new elites took control of the national government, staffing its departments and agencies with their political supporters. As they strengthened their control over the system, they also gradually extended their influence into important subsidiary organizations, such as newspapers, college and university faculties, book publishers, and civic associations. College and university faculties and our major newspapers today are overwhelmingly Democratic; from the 1870s into the 1930s, they were generally Republican. This is one of the factors that cements any realignment in place and gives it the stability to persist over many decades.

One can also identify in all three cases an abrupt change of policy, a broken agreement, or some perceived violation of faith that poisoned relations between the parties, drove them further apart, and closed off possibilities for compromise. The Federalists' passage of the Alien and Sedition Acts (1798), which opponents saw as an attempt to criminalize criticism of the Adams administration, provoked all-out warfare with Jefferson's fledgling party and convinced Jefferson and James Madison that their ultimate goal should be the destruction of the Federalist Party. The Democratic Party's repeal of the Missouri Compromise in 1854 brought the Republican Party into existence and sharpened the sectional conflict by several degrees. In 1932, FDR claimed (falsely in this case) that the bankers and industrialists had caused the Depression by irresponsible speculation in stocks. Because of this violation of trust, he declared that their activities would have to be supervised more closely by federal authorities.

More fundamentally, each of these realignments was carried out and then maintained by one dominant political party. Following the election of 1800, Jefferson's (and later Jackson's) Democratic party defined the parameters of political competition until the outbreak of the sectional crisis in the 1850s. The Republican Party led the nation through the Civil War and maintained its dominant status throughout the post-bellum era of industrial development. In the midst of the Great Depression, FDR's Democratic Party organized the modern system around the politics of public spending and national regulation. The Democrats completed this revolution after World War II when the United States began to assume responsibilities in the international arena commensurate with those it had already assumed in the domestic economic arena.

The dominant parties in each of these eras might be called "regime parties" because they were able to use their political strength to implement and carry forward the basic themes around which these political settlements were organized. Jefferson's party pushed forward the themes of localism, democracy, and expansion; Lincoln's, the themes of union, freedom, and capitalism; FDR's, the themes of national regulation, public spending, and internationalism. In this sense, the United States has rarely had a two-party system but rather a one and one-half party system consisting of a "regime party" and a competitor forced to adapt to its dominant position. These competitors—the Whigs in the 1840s, the Democrats after the Civil War, and the Republicans in the post-war era—occasionally won national elections, but only after accepting the legitimacy of the basic political themes established by the regime party.

The question today, then, is whether or not the party system formed in the 1930s and 1940s is about to exhaust itself in a new upheaval that will lead to some new political alignment around a new constellation of issues. There is little doubt that many of the political signs present in earlier upheavals are increasingly in play today.

The Democratic Party established itself in the 1930s and 1940s as the "regime party" in modern American politics by building majorities around the claims that it pulled the country out of the Depression and won the war against fascism. Democrats won five consecutive presidential elections from 1932 to 1948, comparable to the six straight ones won by Jefferson's party between 1800 and 1820 and the six won by Republicans from 1860 to 1880. Throughout the period from the 1930s into the 1980s, Democrats consistently maintained control over both houses of the U.S. Congress. This electoral strength gave the Democrats solid control over the institutions of the national government.

Given the popularity of FDR and the New Deal, Republicans had little choice but to accept the general contours of the new regime. Following their landslide defeat in 1936, Republicans nominated a succession of presidential candidates—Willkie, Dewey, Eisenhower, and Nixon—who did not challenge New Deal programs but promised only to administer them more effectively. Among Republican candidates between 1940 and 1980, only Barry Goldwater sought to roll back the New Deal, and his defeat in 1964 was taken as evidence of the futility of that strategy.

Over the decades, the Democratic Party has built its coalition around public spending and the recruitment of new groups into the political process, often by promises of new public programs. It has displayed a remarkable capacity to renew itself by adjusting its appeals to the ever-changing political marketplace. In the 1930s, FDR built his coalition around urban workers, farmers, and industrial unions with appeals that grew out of the grim realities of mass unemployment and destitution. By the 1960s, John F. Kennedy and his successors succeeded in broadening the Party's appeal to the middle class and suburban home owners by pushing "quality of life" themes like environmentalism, civil rights, women's rights, and government support for the arts. Later, as private sector unions began to disappear in the 1970s and 1980s, Democrats replaced them in several key states by organizing public sector unions and mobilizing them into their party. In many states, these unions provide the organizational backbone of the Party by supplying votes and money and serving as well-placed advocates for further public spending. The Democratic Party has gradually evolved into a "public sector party" that finds its votes and organizational strength in public sector unions, government employees and contractors, and beneficiaries of government programs.

Many thoughtful observers argue that the New Deal alignment came apart in the 1960s and was replaced by Ronald Reagan's conservative revolution in the 1980s. There is something to be said for this view. Since the 1980 election, Republicans have achieved rough electoral parity with the Democrats, winning five of eight presidential elections and winning control of the House and Senate in roughly half of the elections that have taken place since that time. The Republicans, much in contrast to the Democrats, have organized themselves in recent decades as a "private sector party," winning votes and contributions from individuals and business groups committed to cutting taxes and reducing the size and scope of government.

Despite their electoral successes since the 1980s, Republicans never managed to reverse the flow of political power to Washington and failed to eliminate or substantially reduce any of the New Deal or Great Society social programs. Federal spending on domestic programs grew nearly as quickly under Republican as Democratic administrations. Republicans have on occasion tried to balance the budget or tinker with Social Security and Medicare but were rebuffed by Democrats who accused them of trying to destroy these popular programs. Republican governors and mayors, like their Democratic counterparts, continue to make their pilgrimages to Washington in search of grant money and subsidies for their states and cities, just as members of Congress from both parties run for reelection by pointing to the federal funds they have brought back to their states and districts.

Nor have Republicans had much success in penetrating leading cultural and educational institutions on behalf of ideas that have wide support among voters. College faculties and editorial boards are more resolutely Democratic and liberal today than they were in the 1960s. Republicans have so far been unable to parlay their considerable electoral success into commensurate influence over cultural, journalistic, and educational institutions. Conservatives, in fact, have done something altogether different: they have created their own newspapers, magazines, think tanks and research institutes, and colleges and schools to circulate their ideas. They have, in effect, formed their own "counter-establishment" through which they communicate with their supporters and wage ideological warfare against Democrats. The two parties increasingly live in their own political and philosophical worlds, a fact that obviously drives their members further apart and makes compromises between them ever more difficult to achieve.

This evolution has now produced a volatile and potentially destabilizing alignment between the two major parties, with one rooted in the public sector and the other in the private sector, and with each communicating mainly with its own supporters. In the past, political parties were coalitions of private interests seeking influence over government in order to facilitate their growth within the private economy. This was true of early party conflicts that pitted commerce against agriculture or the later splits between slavery and free labor or business against organized labor. The regional and sectional conflicts of the past were also of this character. This was in keeping with the small government bias of the Constitution in which the government itself was never supposed to emerge as a political interest in its own right.

The conflict today between Democrats and Republicans increasingly pits public sector unions, government employees and contractors, and beneficiaries of government programs against middle-class taxpayers and business interests large and small. In states where public spending is high and public sector unions are strong, as in New York, California, Illinois, and Connecticut, Democrats have gained control; where public sector interests are weak or poorly organized, as in most of the states across the south and southwest, Republicans have the edge. This configuration, when added up across the nation, has produced a series of electoral stand-offs in recent decades between the red and blue states that have been decided by a handful of swing states moving in one direction or the other.

This impasse between the two parties signals the end game for the system of politics that originated in the 1930s and 1940s. As the "regime party," the Democrats are in the more vulnerable position because they have built their coalition around public spending, public debt, and publicly guaranteed credit, all sources of funds that appear to be reaching their limits. The end game for the New Deal system, and for the Democrats as our "regime party," will arrive when those limits are reached or passed.

This point will arrive fairly soon for the following reasons: (1) unsustainable debt; (2) public promises that cannot be fulfilled; (3) stagnation and slow growth; and (4) political paralysis. The last point is important because it means that the parties will fail to agree on any preemptive solutions to the above problems until they reach a point of crisis.

1. Everyone is aware of the accumulated U.S. debt: $16 trillion by the end of 2012, which amounts to more than the nation's Gross Domestic Product of about $15.5 trillion. Of this debt, about $11 trillion rests in public hands and the remainder is in government accounts. This year, the federal government will pay about $275 billion in interest payments on the debt, or about 6 percent of a federal budget of $3.8 trillion. The interest on publicly held debt (which comes to another $200 billion annually) is paid with government "IOU's" that will be redeemed in the future out of tax revenues. Interest rates are at a historically low point, a condition that is unlikely to last much longer. It is possible that within a few years, if creditors demand higher rates to purchase our debt, our government could be spending as much as 20 percent of its revenues on interest payments. Those payments must be made at the expense of existing programs, including defense, Medicaid, Medicare, education, and Social Security. No one can foretell when credit markets may decide that our debt is too risky to hold at these interest rates. Since foreign governments hold more than a third of our public debt, they could decide as a matter of policy to sell

U.S. debt and invest their resources elsewhere. Such an event in and of itself would precipitate a crisis in our public accounts.

The above does not begin to address all of the unstated or "unofficial" liabilities of the U.S. government, such as promises made to Social Security and Medicare beneficiaries and sums needed to back up federal mortgage guarantees. Some estimate that these liabilities could run as high as $50 trillion. In addition, many state governments have had difficulty balancing their budgets, and some have been able to do so only because of large transfers from the federal government in the 2009 stimulus package and increased payments for education, transportation, and social services in recent federal budgets. State employee pension programs are notoriously underfunded because states have deferred annual payments in order to meet other pressing obligations and the returns on these funds have been well below actuarial assumptions. A recent study suggested that the real value of these obligations across the country is more than $5 trillion while states have put aside only about one-third of this amount in current trust funds. What will the states do when employees line up to collect payments to which they feel they are entitled?

2. In addition to such debt and credit issues, the finances of federal entitlement programs are similarly approaching a point of crisis and insolvency. The most expensive entitlement programs are for old age pensions (Social Security) and health care (Medicare). Currently the U.S. government spends about $725 billion annually on Social Security and $650 billion on Medicare, or about $1.4 trillion on the two program combined, or more than one-third of total federal expenditures. There are now about 45 million people eligible for Medicare and 44

million for Social Security. These numbers are about to explode due to the impending retirement of the "baby boom" generation, or those born between the years 1946 and 1963. There are currently between 75 and 80 million baby boomers, the leading edge of which reached age 65 in 2011. By the year 2025, there will be close to 80 million Americans, and perhaps several million more, who will be eligible to receive benefits under Social Security and Medicare. Given their likely longevity, they will be collecting benefits for years into the future. Meanwhile, they will be retiring from the work force almost as quickly as new entrants are joining. There are now about 125 million people working on a full-time basis in the United States, a number that is expected to grow far more slowly each year than the number of new retirees. In a dozen years or so, we may have as many as 80 million people collecting old age benefits against a working population of 130 or 135 million, and in a fiscal situation in which the federal government is already deeply in the red. These promises cannot be fulfilled without bankrupting the government or the taxpayers, or without strangling the private economy with excessive taxes. This situation by itself has the potential to create a political upheaval.

One might ask why our government has not made preparations for a development that has been in the making for the past sixty-five years. Far from making preparations for this event, the political authorities have done several things in recent years to make the problem even more acute. In 2001, the Congress passed an expensive prescription benefit program for seniors without providing the funds to pay for it. Many blame President George W. Bush and the Republican Congress for this, but it was not entirely their fault alone, since the Democrats in Congress proposed an even more expensive program than the one that was eventually passed. In 2009, President Obama, with a Democratic Congress, passed a new health care entitlement program to guarantee coverage for the 40 million or so Americans without health insurance, but paying for it by taking $50 billion per year from Medicare, thus further stretching a system that was already on the path to insolvency. In addition, the U.S. government has taken annual surpluses from the Social Security Trust Fund and applied them to deficits arising in the overall federal budget. This accounts for a large share of the $5 trillion or so in debt held internally by the government. Beginning in 2009, the Social Security Trust Fund began to run a deficit, and will remain in deficit for at least another twenty years until the baby boom generation passes through the system. What this means is that the U.S. government will have to make up the funds it has borrowed from the Trust Fund from annual tax revenues.

3. Then there is the problem of stagnating economic growth. The United States needs a rapidly growing economy to produce the income and wealth to pay for these expensive government programs. After all, tax revenues have to be taken from the private sector; the public sector does not generate wealth on its own. Yet, decade by decade, growth has been slowing down in the United States. During the 1950s and 1960s, real GDP grew by an average of 4.3 percent per year, but during the decade of the 1970s, that rate fell to 3.7 percent. It fell further in the 1980s to 3.5 percent, and during the 1990s to 3.2 percent. Following the technology "bust" and recession of 2000, GDP grew from 2000 to 2008 by a rate of 2.6 percent per year, but if we factor in the recession of 2008 and 2009, GDP grew at a rate of 1.7 percent per year for the whole decade of 2000 to 2009. Now, in the past three years, we have bounced out of a very steep recession

with only tepid rates of growth of around 2 percent per year. Forecasters expect this trend to continue for years into the future, partly owing to the burdens of debt and the need to pay it down.

There are many possible reasons for this slowdown in growth. A mature economy tends to grow at a slower rate than an emerging economy. Some suggest that the rate of technological progress has slowed down over the past thirty or forty years, contributing to the slowdown in growth. Whatever the cause, long-run stagnation will make it impossible to pay off the promises the federal government has made.

4. But isn't it possible for Congress and the President to step in now to formulate a strategy to deal with these problems before they reach a crisis point? Various proposals have been set forth: the Bowles-Simpson plan, for example, and other plans to reduce the budget deficit over a ten-year period. To their credit, Republicans in Congress have stepped forward with a plan to reform Medicare and Medicaid and to re-write the tax code so that it encourages economic growth. Thus far, the Democrats have been silent. In any case, such proposals are unlikely to be adopted. For one thing, the problems are too large to be dealt with in any preemptive fashion. The prospect of cutting the federal budget by more than a third is hard to contemplate for politicians who have grown up in an environment of affluence and abundant resources. In addition, it is unrealistic to look to our political process to solve a problem that it has been instrumental in creating.

The regime of public spending has at last drawn so many groups into the public arena in search of public dollars that it has paralyzed the political process and driven governments to the edge of bankruptcy. These groups are widely varied: trade associations, educational lobbies, public employee unions, government contractors, ideological and advocacy organizations, health-care providers, hospital associations that earn revenues from Medicare and Medicaid programs, and the like. These are what economists call rent-seeking groups because they are concerned with the distribution of resources rather than with the creation of wealth. They consume rather than create wealth. These groups are highly influential in the political process because they are willing to invest large sums in lobbying and election campaigns in order to protect their sources of income. While rent-seeking groups can be found in both political parties, the largest and most influential of them (at least on the spending side) have congregated within the Democratic Party. To expand on what was said earlier, one might describe the Democratic Party as a coalition of rent-seekers.

Rent-seeking coalitions have little interest in moderating their demands in the interests of the broader economy because, as their leaders reason, the economy will be little affected by the small share of it to which they are laying claim. In addition, they calculate that if they do not take the money, then someone else will—and so they are not inclined to be "fools" for the public interest. But since the leaders of all rent-seeking groups think this way, the interest group system as a whole operates with little concern for the requirements of economic growth and wealth generation. This is one reason why, in times of crisis, rent-seeking coalitions demand tax increases to pay for their programs instead of recommending policies to accelerate growth.

The late economist Mancur Olson has argued that economies tend to grow more slowly as rent-seeking coalitions become pervasive and ubiquitous, since they divert resources from wealth-creating to wealth-consuming uses. This is one reason, he argues, why the United States grew so rapidly in the nineteenth century, and why West Germany and Japan grew so rapidly in the two or three decades after World War II. At such times, these economies were open to investment and entrepreneurship, and, as a consequence, they enjoyed historically high rates of growth. With the passage of time, all of these systems were gradually encumbered by coalitions seeking benefits through the state. Political paralysis and slow growth, Olson argues, are by-products of political systems captured by rent-seeking coalitions. These groups, operating collectively, can block any overall effort to cut spending or to address the problems of deficits and debt.

The political problem is compounded because the two political parties have diverged to a point unknown in our lifetimes and not seen in America since the upheavals of the 1850s. In the post-war era, during the 1950s and 1960s, it was possible to pass bipartisan legislation with majorities or near majorities of both parties. The Civil Rights Bill of 1964 was passed with a coalition of northern Democrats and Republicans against the opposition of Democrats in the south. Medicare was likewise passed with bipartisan majorities. During the 1970s, the two parties began to diverge into liberal and conservative wings in a process that has continued to the point where, today, there is no ideological overlap between the two congressional parties—that is, the most conservative Democrat is more liberal than the most liberal Republican. Thus the two parties must increasingly bargain like foreign adversaries who fundamentally distrust one another, rather as the pro- and anti-slavery forces bargained during the 1850s. Because of this divergence, there will be no "grand bargain" or preemptive solution to America's fiscal crisis.

What, then, is likely to happen? The United States will lurch forward for a few years yet, borrowing still more money to finance our public programs and putting off, for a time, any serious measures to address the problems of spending and debt until some event intervenes to force our hand. The United States has placed itself in a position in which it is vulnerable to any number of unforeseen and uncontrollable events. The bond markets could revolt against increasing levels of debt. Interest rates could rise to ruinous levels. A major bank or two might fail, precipitating a new financial crisis. A war or revolution in the Middle East could cause a spike in oil prices. Terrorists might strike again. We could face a new recession before we have fully recovered from the last one. Europe could go into recession as a result of its own debt crisis, thereby curbing the demand for American exports. Because the United States is already skating on thin ice with little room to maneuver, any or all of these events would bring the current system to a point of crisis where Congress would have to slash spending and renegotiate promises it has made. At this point the United States would enter uncharted political territory.

This would be the ultimate challenge for a political regime organized around public spending and debt. It would immediately lead to a highly charged political situation in which incumbents are voted out of office, interest groups battle to protect their pieces of the budget, and the political parties struggle to keep their electoral coalitions intact. As this process unfolds, Americans may then witness the kinds of events not seen in this country since the 1930s or, even, the 1850s and 1860s: protesters invading the U.S. Capitol, politicians refusing to leave office after they have lost elections, defiance of the Supreme Court, the emergence of new leaders, and, possibly, the formation of new political parties. All of this can be expected from a process in which an entrenched system of politics withers and dies and a new one is gradually organized to take its place.

Does the "fourth revolution" imply the "end of America," as some have suggested? Not necessarily, though one must acknowledge the possibility that this upheaval might end badly, perhaps in an extended period of political conflict and paralysis that yields no constructive outcome. Yet, based on the evidence of the three previous revolutions, American voters are unlikely to support for very long any party that fails to enhance their standard of living or the nation's position in the world.

If the three previous revolutions offer any lessons, then there is every chance that the United States will emerge from this crisis with new momentum to develop its economy and provide leadership for the world.

President Obama came to office in 2008 promising to be all things to all people, or at least many things to many people. Above all, he was determined to be a revolutionary president, one who ushered in a new era of progress guided by an activist government. He announced his candidacy in Springfield, Illinois, thus identifying with Abraham Lincoln. He won the endorsement of the Kennedy family as the heir apparent of JFK's legacy. When he came to office, he called on memories of FDR with the idea that he (like FDR) would guide the nation out of a depression. More recently, he adopted the mantle of Theodore Roosevelt and his program for a "new nationalism." Of late he has sounded like Harry Truman running against a "do nothing" Congress. Has he learned the right lessons from history?

Unfortunately, in trying to emulate FDR and his other predecessors, who were operating under far different circumstances, President Obama made all of our current problems worse. His stimulus and budget packages added to the national debt without doing anything to stimulate economic growth. He spent his first two years passing an expensive health-care bill instead of focusing on steps to promote recovery and growth. By ramming all of these measures through on narrowly partisan votes, he destroyed the comity between the parties. On the health-care bill, he broke the longstanding agreement between the parties that important pieces of social legislation should be passed on a bipartisan basis. He has thus managed to divide the public without doing much to solve the problems he was elected to address.

Many analysts expect President Obama to be reelected this November. Perhaps the odds favor him. After all, it is difficult to unseat an incumbent. Yet, the economy is still weak, his policies have not succeeded in turning it around, and he is not widely popular. No matter how it turns out, this year's presidential election is likely to sharpen, rather than to resolve, political divisions in the United States. Despite all this, President Obama is unshaken in his presumption that he is a herald of a new era, a revolutionary on the models of Jefferson, Lincoln, and FDR. But is it possible that he will instead turn out to be something much different, a modern-day Adams, Buchanan, or Hoover—that is, the last representative of a disintegrating order? Such a denouement is not only possible but, in view of our situation, more and more likely.

The Lessons of Culture

Roger Kimball

*We sit by and watch the Barbarian. We tolerate him. In
the long stretches of peace, we are not afraid. We are
tickled by his reverence, his comic inversion of our old
certitudes and our fixed creeds refreshes us: we laugh. But
as we laugh, we are watched by large and awful faces from
beyond. And on these faces, there is no smile.*

—Hilaire Belloc on the ruins of Timgad

*If we want things to stay as they are, things will have to
change."*

—Tancredi, in Lampedusa's *The Leopard*

*The simple process of preserving our present civilization
is supremely complex, and demands incalculably subtle
powers.*

—José Ortega y Gasset

THE LESSONS OF CULTURE: What are they? One of the
leitmotifs threading its way through the essays that
compose "Future Tense" is the recognition that we are
living in the midst of one of those "plastic moments" that
Karl Marx talked about. Future *tense:* not just subsequent,
but also fraught. To revise an old song: Will there always
be an England? That "will there always be ..." is every-

where on our lips, in our hearts. And it's not just England we worry about. The law; the economy; the political prospects; changes in our intellectual habits wrought by changes in our technology; the destiny that is demography: America, the West, indeed the entire world in the early years of the twenty-first century, seems curiously unsettled. Things we had taken for granted seem suddenly up for grabs in some fundamental if still-difficult-to-grasp way. Fissures open among the confidences we had always assumed—in "the market," in national identity, in the basics of social order and cultural value. Future tense: the always hazardous art of cultural prognostication seems brittler now, more uneasy, more tentative.

Granted, the parochial assumption of present disruption is a hardy perennial. As Gibbon observed in *The Decline and Fall of the Roman Empire,* "There exists in human nature a strong propensity to depreciate the advantages, and to magnify the evils, of the present times." But we know from history (including the history that Gibbon gave us) that there are times when that natural propensity has colluded seamlessly with the actual facts. In *Thoughts on the Cause of the Present Discontents,* Burke (as usual) got it exactly right:

> To complain of the age we live in, to murmur at the present possessors of power, to lament the past, to conceive extravagant hopes of the future, are the common dispositions of the greatest part of mankind; indeed the necessary effects of the ignorance and levity of the vulgar. Such complaints and humours have existed in all times; yet as all times have not been alike, true political sagacity manifests itself, in distinguishing that complaint which only characterizes the general infirmity of human nature, from those which are symptoms of the particular distemperature of our own air and season.

A book called *Thoughts on the Cause of the Present Discontents* will always be pertinent. Burke's point is that whereas some discontents are part of the human condition, others are part of the conditions humans forge for themselves. It is the latter, and the pressure or intrusion of the former upon the latter, we have sought to highlight in this series of essays.

Is there something unique, or at least distinctively different, about the economic crisis that began in 2008, was supposed to have evaporated by now, but that is lingering on if not getting worse? Has the ideology of transnational progressivism made such inroads among political elites that it threatens American self-determination and individual liberty? (I think of Burke again: "It was soon discovered, that the forms of a free, and the ends of an arbitrary Government, were things not altogether incompatible.") Is America on the brink (or even beyond the brink) of a "fourth revolution"—following on the original revolution of American Independence, the Civil War, and the revolution wrought by FDR's New Deal—are we, another eighty years on, facing a new revolution that will fundamentally reshape political and cultural life in this country? These are among the questions we have conjured with in "Future Tense." Last month, Charles Murray asked whether "a major stream of artistic accomplishment can be produced by a society that is geriatric [as ours, increasingly, is]? By a society that is secular? By an advanced welfare state?" We do not know the answers to those questions, Mr. Murray observed, because "we are facing unprecedented situations."

> We have never observed a great civilization with a population as old as the United States will have in the twenty-first century; we have never observed a great civilization that is

as secular as we are apparently going to become; and we have had only half a century of experience with advanced welfare states.

Which leaves us—where? In 1911, the poet-philosopher T. E. Hulme observed that "there must be one word in the language spelt in capital letters. For a long time, and still for sane people, the word was God. Then one became bored with the letter 'G,' and went on to 'R,' and for a hundred years it was Reason, and now all the best people take off their hats and lower their voices when they speak of Life." I think Hulme was on to something, both in his observation about the inveterate habit of reverence and the choice that sanity dictates. I wonder, though, whether we as a culture haven't shifted our attention from "L" for "Life" to "E" for "Egalitarianism" or "P" for "Political Correctness."

It is noteworthy, in any event, to what extent certain key words live in a state of existential diminishment. Consider the word "Gentleman." It was not so long ago that it named a critical moral-social-cultural aspiration. What happened to the phenomenon it named? Or think of the word "respectable." It too has become what the philosopher David Stove called a "smile word," that is, a word that names a forgotten or neglected or out-of-fashion social virtue that we might remember but no longer publicly practice. The *word* still exists, but the reality has been ironized out of serious discussion. It is hard to use straight. Just as it would be difficult to call someone "respectable" today without silently adding a dollop of irony, so it is with the word "gentleman."

Leo Strauss made the witty observation that the word "virtue," which once referred to the manliness of a man, had come to refer primarily to the chastity of a woman. We've moved on from that, of course. Chastity was for centuries a prime theme of Western dramatic art even as it was an obsession of Western culture. Who can even pronounce the word these days without a knowing smile? And as for manliness, well, the philosopher Harvey Mansfield wrote an entire book diagnosing (and lamenting) its mutation into ironized irrelevance.

Here's the question: Absent the guiding stringencies of manliness, which are also the tonic assumptions of cultural confidence, how should we understand "the lessons of culture"? In his reflections on Pericles for "Future Tense," Victor Davis Hanson noted that "the unabashed confidence of Pericles in his own civilization and national ethos . . . were once gold standards for unapologetic Western democratic rhetoricians." And not only rhetoricians, but for Western democracies *tout court*. Pericles, Mr. Hanson observes, reminds us that "should a great culture not feel that its values and achievements are exceptional," then no one else will either. The eclipse of that fundamental confidence is "injurious" to small and insignificant states, but "fatal" to states, like the United States, with aspirations to global leadership.

And where does that leave us? In one of his essays on humanism, T. S. Eliot observed that when we "boil down Horace, the Elgin Marbles, St. Francis, and Goethe" the result will be "pretty thin soup." "Culture," he concluded, "is not enough, even though nothing is enough without culture." In other words, culture is more than a parade of names, a first prize in the game of "cultural literacy." Let me me return to and elaborate on Mr. Hanson's observations about Pericles. What lessons does the great Greek statesman have for us today? Does his example as a leader of the Athenians at the beginning of the Peloponnesian War have a special pertinence for us as we think about "the lessons of culture"?

To answer these questions, one first wants to know: What is it that Pericles stood for? To what sort of society was he pointing? What way of life, what vision of the human good did he propound?

In his history of the Peloponnesian War, Thucydides recounts the public funeral oration that Pericles, as commander of the army and first citizen of Athens, delivered to commemorate those fallen after the first year—the first of twenty-seven years, be it noted—of war with Sparta. As Mr. Hanson reminds us, the short speech is deservedly one of the most famous in history.

The funeral oration outlines the advantages of Athenian democracy, a bold new system of government that was not simply a political arrangement but a way of life. There were two keynotes to that way of life: freedom and tolerance on the one hand, responsible behavior and attention to duty on the other.

The two go together. We Athenians, Pericles said, are "free and tolerant in our private lives; but in public affairs we keep to the law"—including, he added in an important proviso, "those unwritten laws," like the lawlike commands of taste, manners, and morals—"which it is an acknowledged shame to break." Freedom and tolerance, Pericles suggested, were blossoms supported by roots that reached deep into the soil of duty. Burke again: "Manners are of more importance than law.... The law touches us but here and there and now and then. Manners are what vex or soothe, corrupt or purify, exalt or debase, barbarize or refine us, by a constant, steady, uniform and insensible operation like that of the air we breathe in."

Athens had become the envy of the world, partly because of its wealth, partly because of its splendor, partly because of the freedom enjoyed by its citizens. Athens' navy was unrivaled, its empire unparalleled, its civic and cultural institutions unequalled. The city was "open to the world," a cosmopolitan center. Political life was "free and open," as was private life: "We do not get into a state with our next-door neighbor," Pericles said, "if he enjoys himself in his own way."

Of course, from the perspective of twenty-first-century America, democracy in Athens may seem limited and imperfect. Women were entirely excluded from citizenship in Athens, and there was a large slave class that underwrote the material freedom of Athens' citizens. These things must be acknowledged. But must they be apologized for? Whenever fifth-century Athens is mentioned these days, it seems that what is stressed is not the achievement of Athenian democracy but its limitations.

To my mind, concentrating on the limitations of Athenian democracy is like complaining that the Wright brothers neglected to provide transatlantic service with their airplanes. The extraordinary achievement of Athens was to formulate the ideal of equality before the law. To be sure, that ideal was not perfectly instantiated in Athens. Perhaps it never will be perfectly instantiated, it being in the nature of ideals to inspire emulation but also to exceed it.

The point to bear in mind is that both the ideal of equality before the law and the cultivation of an open, tolerant society were new. They made Athens the model of democracy for all the republics that sought to follow the path of freedom—just as America is the model of freedom today. Pericles was right to boast that "Future ages will wonder at us, as the present age wonders at us now." To continue the theme of aviation, we might say that in Athens, after innumerable trials elsewhere, democracy finally managed to get off the ground and stay aloft. In Periclean Athens what mattered in assuming public responsibility, as Pericles said, was "not membership in a particular class, but the actual ability which the man possesses." To an extraordinary extent, within the limits of its franchise, Athens lived up to that ideal.

It is also worth noting that life in Athens was not only free but also full. Here we come to the lessons of culture. When the day's work was done, Pericles boasted, Athenians turned not simply to private pleasure but also to ennobling recreation "of all kinds for our spirits." For the Age of Pericles was also the age of the great dramatists, the age of Socrates, the great artist Phidias, and others. Freedom, skill, and ambition conspired to make Athens a cultural as well as a political paragon.

A recurrent theme of the funeral oration is the importance of sound judgment, what Aristotle codified as the manly virtue of prudence. The blessing of freedom requires the ballast of duty, and informed judgment is the indispensable handmaiden of duty. It also requires courage: the indispensable virtue, as Aristotle pointed out, because it makes the practice of all the other virtues possible. A free society is one that nurtures the existential slack that tolerance and openness generate. Chaos and anarchy are forestalled by the intervention of politics in the highest sense of the term: deliberation and decision about securing the good life. When it comes to cultural activities, Pericles said, Athenians had learned to love beauty with moderation—the Greek word is *euteleias*, "without extravagance"—and to pursue philosophy and the life of the mind "without effeminacy," *aneu malakias*. The lessons of culture were to be ennoblements of life, not an escape from its burdens.

The exercise of sound judgment was required in other spheres as well. In their conduct of policy, Athenians strove to be bold, but prudent, i.e., effective. "We are,"

Pericles wrote, "capable at the same time of taking risks and of estimating them beforehand." The exercise of sound judgment was not simply an intellectual accomplishment; it was the tithe of citizenship. "We do not say that a man who takes no interest in politics is a man who minds his own business," Pericles observed, "we say that he has no business here at all."

Pericles did not mean that every citizen had to be a politician. What he meant was that all citizens had a common stake in the commonwealth of the city. And that common stake brought with it common responsibilities as well as common privileges. At a time when everyone is clamoring for his or her "rights"—when new "rights" pop up like mushrooms after a rain—it is worth remembering that every right carries with it a corresponding duty. We enjoy certain rights because we discharge corresponding responsibilities. Some rights may be inalienable; none is without a price.

Something similar can be said about democracy. Today, the word "democracy" and its cognates are often used as fancy synonyms for mediocrity. When we read about plans to "democratize" education or the arts or athletics, we know that is shorthand for plans to eviscerate those activities, for lowering standards, and pursuing them as instruments of racial or sexual redress or some other form of social engineering. Alexis de Tocqueville was right to warn about the dangers of generalizing the principle of equality that underlies democracy. Universalized, the principle of equality leads to egalitarianism, the ideology of equality.

The problem today is that the egalitarian imperative threatens to overwhelm that other great social impulse, the impulse to achieve, to excel, to surpass: "always to be best and to rise above others," as Homer put it in one classic expression of the agonistic spirit. Radical egalitarianism—egalitarianism uncorrected by the aspirations of excellence—would have us pretend that there are no important distinctions among people; where the pretense is impossible, it would have us enact compensatory programs to minimize, or at least to paper over, the differences. The results are a vast increase in self-deception, cultural degradation, and bureaucratic meddlesomeness: the reign, in short, of political correctness. It is refreshing to turn to Pericles and remind ourselves that a passion for democracy need not entail the pursuit of mediocrity. Democracy is a high-maintenance form of government. Freedom requires disciplined restraint and circumspection if it is to flourish. Athenian democracy was animated by freedom, above all the freedom to excel, and it inspired in citizens both a healthy competitive spirit and "shame," as Pericles said, at the prospect of "falling below a certain standard."

In all this, Pericles noted, Athens was "an education to Greece," a model for its neighbors. At the moment he spoke, at the beginning of a long and ultimately disastrous war, his words must have had special resonance. In celebrating what the Athenians had achieved, he was also reminding them of all they stood to lose. His funeral oration was therefore not only an elegy but also a plea for resoluteness and a call to arms. It is a call that resonates with special significance now that the United States and indeed all of what used to be called Christendom is under siege. Pericles was right: The open society depends upon the interdiction of forces calculated to destroy it. "We who remain behind," he said, "may hope to be spared the fate [of the fallen], but must resolve to keep the same daring spirit against the foe."

The view of society and the individual's responsibility that Pericles put forward was rooted in tradition but oriented toward the future. He did not think much of the custom of public funeral orations, he said, but he felt bound to observe it: "This institution was set up and approved by our forefathers, and it is my duty to follow the tradition." At the same time Pericles reminds us of the claims of the future by stressing the future's main emissaries: the children of Athens. "It is impossible," he suggests, "for a man to put forward fair and honest views about our affairs if he has not ... children whose lives are at stake."

The vision of society that Pericles articulated in the funeral oration has exercised a permanent fascination on the political imagination of the West. Although occasionally lost sight of, it has always returned to inspire apostles of freedom and tolerance. But it is imperative that we understand that the view of society that Pericles described is not inevitable. It represents a choice—a choice, moreover, that must constantly be renewed. It is one version of the good life for man. There are other, competing versions that we would find distinctly less attractive. In the West, Pericles' vision, modified by time and circumstance, has proven to be a peculiarly powerful one. It was absorbed by Christendom in the eighteenth century and helped to inform the democratic principles that undergird British and American democracy.

But we would be untrue to Pericles' counsel of vigilance were we to think that some of the alternatives to this vision were incapable of inspiring strong allegiance. This was true when Pericles spoke. His entire speech presupposes the contrast between the Athenian way of life and another that was inimical to it. It continues to be true. The spectacle of radical Islamists dancing joyfully in the street whenever news of a terrorist atrocity breaks reminds us of that fact.

Indeed, the status of Pericles' vision of society as one alternative among others was dramatically sharpened by the events of September 11. For that attack was not simply an attack on symbols of American capitalism or American military might. Nor was it just a terrorist attack on American citizens. It was all those things and more. It was an attack on the idea of America as a liberal democratic society, which means that it was an attack on an idea of society that had one of its primary sources in the ideals enunciated by Pericles. Shortly after the attacks, Benjamin Netanyahu made the observation that 9/11 was a salvo in "a war to reverse the triumph of the West." Netanyahu's words should be constantly borne in mind lest the emollient tide of rationalization blunt the angry reality of those attacks.

Many illusions were challenged on September 11. One illusion concerns the fantasies of academic multiculturalists, so-called. I say "so-called" because what goes under the name of multiculturalism in our colleges and universities today is really a polysyllabic form of mono-culturalism fueled by ideological hatred. Genuine multiculturalism involves a great deal of work, beginning, say, with the arduous task of learning other languages, something most of those who call themselves multiculturalists are conspicuously loath to do.

Think of the fatuous attack on "dead white European males" that stands at the center of the academic multiculturalist enterprise. For a specimen of that maligned species, one could hardly do better than Pericles. Not only is he a dead white European male, but he is one who embodied in his life and aspirations an ideal of humanity completely at odds with academic multiculturalism. He was patriarchal, militarist, elitist, and Eurocentric. He exhibited a manly confidence in the values of his culture that was as inspiring as it was indispensable.

Did Pericles survive September 11? Even now, a decade later, it is too soon to say which way the rhetorical chips will ultimately fall. The elimination of Osama bin Laden by a team of Navy SEALs last year marked the end of a chapter, but it was quickly absorbed into a larger metabolism of doubt. There are few signs that America remains prepared to follow through on its promise to eradicate terrorism and hold responsible those states that sponsor, finance, or abet it. There are even fewer signs that America, or the West generally, is prepared to stand up for its own cultural and political legacy in the face of the existential threats that besiege it: Islamism and its encroaching effort to establish Sharia law the world over as well as that potpourri of enervating imperatives that congregate under the banner of transnational progressivism.

The hollowness of the left-liberal wisdom about the war brings me to another illusion that was challenged by the events of 9/11. I mean the illusion that the world is basically a benevolent, freedom-loving place, and that if only other people had enough education, safe sex, and access to National Public Radio, they would become pacific celebrants of democracy and tolerance. This is the temptation of utopia—Greek for "nowhere"—and it must be acknowledged that America's fortunate geographical position in the world has long encouraged certain versions of this temptation. The extraordinary growth of America's wealth and military power in the twentieth-century—like Athens' great wealth and power in the fifth-century B.C.— has kept the wolf from the door and the marauder from our throats. They have also abetted the illusion of invulnerability. But increased international mobility and the widespread dissemination of technological know-how have conspired to neutralize or at least attenuate those advantages. And let's not forget the world-wide economic crisis that, since 2008, has introduced a new current of anxious uncertainty into our deliberations about the future. September 11, which brought the destruction of war to American soil for the first time since the war of 1812, made it abundantly clear that we have implacable enemies, enemies we cannot hide from, effectively appease, or negotiate with, enemies that will struggle to the death to destroy us. The still percolating economic dégringolade should remind us that the spectacular wealth of the West is an achievement, not a birthright. As Robert Heinlein wisely observed,

> Throughout history, poverty is the normal condition of man. Advances which permit this norm to be exceeded— here and there, now and then—are the work of an extremely small minority, frequently despised, often condemned, and almost always opposed by all right-thinking people. Whenever this tiny minority is kept from creating, or (as sometimes happens) is driven out of a society, the people then slip back into abject poverty.

A third illusion that was challenged on September 11 concerns the morality of power. It has been fashionable among trendy academics, CNN commentators, and other armchair utopians to pretend that the use of power by the powerful is, by definition, evil. Violence on the part of anyone claiming to be a victim was excused as the product of "frustration" or "rage"—emotions that for mysterious reasons are held to be exonerating for the dispossessed but incriminating when exhibited by legitimate authority. Hence the ponderous scramble to uncover "root causes": that is, the search for sociological alibis that might absolve the perpetrators of evil from the inconveniences of guilt. As the French philosopher Charles Péguy put it: "Surrender is essentially an operation by means of which we set about explaining instead of acting."

This favorite liberal pastime has not been abandoned, but it looks increasingly rancid. As the commentator Jonathan Rauch wittily put it shortly after the terrorist attacks, the cause of terrorism is terrorists. September 11 reminded us that with power comes responsibility. Power without resolution is perceived as weakness, and weakness is always dangerously provocative. In the aftermath of September 11, we in the West were often cautioned against exciting Islamic rage. My own feeling is that it is salutary for our allies and our enemies alike to understand that American rage, too, is an unpleasant thing. Pericles commended the Athenians on their "adventurous" spirit that had "forced an entry into every sea and into every land." Everywhere, he noted, Athens "left behind . . . everlasting memorials of good done to our friends or suffering inflicted on our enemies."

Since the 1970s, we have tended to flinch from such frank talk; we shy away from talk of forcing anyone to do anything; we seem ashamed of acknowledging that we have enemies let alone acknowledging that we wish them ill; we are embarrassed alike by the perquisites and the obligations of power. Such squeamishness is precisely part of the "effeminacy" against which Pericles warned. We desperately wish to be liked. We forget that true affection depends upon respect.

What, finally, are the lessons of culture? One lesson concerns the proper place of culture in the economy of life. The critic Clement Greenberg, arguing for the importance of disinterested aesthetic experience, was no doubt correct when he argued that "a poor life is lived by any one who doesn't regularly take time out to stand and gaze, or sit and listen, or touch, or smell, or brood, without any further end in mind, simply for the satisfaction gotten from that which is gazed at, listened to, touched, smelled, or brooded upon." At the same time, Greenberg stressed that "there are, of course, more important things than art: life itself, what actually happens to you. This may sound silly, but I have to say it, given what I've heard art-silly people say all my life. . . . Art shouldn't be overrated." One thinks of Dostoyevsky's exclamation that "incredible as it may seem, the day will come when man will quarrel more fiercely about art than about God." Are we there yet?

Another lesson concerns the fragility of civilization. As Evelyn Waugh noted in the dark days of the late 1930s,

> barbarism is never finally defeated; given propitious circumstances, men and women who seem quite orderly will commit every conceivable atrocity. The danger does not come merely from habitual hooligans; we are all potential recruits for anarchy. Unremitting effort is needed to keep men living together at peace; there is only a margin of energy left over for experiment, however beneficent. Once the prisons of the mind have been opened, the orgy is on. . . . The work of preserving society is sometimes onerous, sometimes almost effortless. The more elaborate the society, the more vulnerable it is to attack, and the more complete its collapse in case of defeat. At a time like the present it is notably precarious. If it falls we shall see not merely the dissolution of a few joint-stock corporations, but of the spiritual and material achievements of our history.

It is a prime lesson of culture to acquaint us with those facts. "History," Walter Bagehot wrote in *Physics and Politics,* his clear-eyed paean to liberal democracy, "is strewn with the wrecks of nations which have gained a little pro-gressiveness at the cost of a great deal of hard manliness, and have thus prepared themselves for destruction as soon as the movements of the world gave a chance for it." Cul-ture is a precious inheritance, immeasurably more difficult to achieve than to destroy, and, once destroyed, almost irretrievable. It's not at all clear that we have learned the lesson, though wise men from before the time of Pericles have sought to bring us that sobering news.

Contributors

Anthony Daniels is the Dietrich Weismann Fellow at the Manhattan Institute and a former doctor who has worked around the globe, spending time across Africa and in his native England. He writes a column for the *London Spectator* and frequently contributes to the *Daily Telegraph*, *The New Criterion*, and *The Times*. His many books include *In Praise of Prejudice: The Necessity of Preconceived Ideas* (2007) and *The New Vichy Syndrome: Why European Intellectuals Surrender to Barbarism* (2010).

Victor Davis Hanson, a National Humanities Medal and Bradley Prize winner, is the Martin and Illie Anderson Senior Fellow in Residence in Classics and Military History at the Hoover Institution. He most recent books include *The Father of Us All: War and History, Ancient and Modern* (2011) and *The End of Sparta: A Novel* (2011).

David Bentley Hart is an Eastern Orthodox theologian, philosopher, and cultural commentator. He has held the Robert J. Randall Chair in Christian Culture at Providence College and has taught at the University of Virginia and Duke Divinity School, among other institutions. He is the author of several books, including *Atheist Delusions: The Christian Revolution and Its Fashionable Enemies* (2010), which won the 2011 Michael Ramsey Prize for Theological Writing.

Roger Kimball is the Editor & Publisher of *The New Criterion*, and President and Publisher of Encounter Books. He has written extensively for publications in both the United States and England including *The Times Literary Supplement, The Wall Street Journal, The Weekly Standard, The American Spectator,* and more. He has also authored numerous books, most recently *The Rape of the Masters: How Political Correctness Sabotages Art* (2004) and *The Fortunes of Permanence: Culture and Anarchy in an Age of Amnesia* (2012).

Michael J. Lewis is a Faison-Pierson-Stoddard Professor of Art at Williams College. He is the author of *Gothic Revival* (2002) and *American Art & Architecture* (2006). His book *August Reichensperger: The Politics of the German Gothic Revival* (1993) was awarded the Alice Davis Hitchcock Book Award by the Society of Architectural Historians. His writing has appeared in *Commentary, The Wall Street Journal,* and *The New Criterion.*

Andrew C. McCarthy is a Senior Fellow at the National Review Institute and former Assistant United States Attorney. He writes frequently for *National Review* and *Commentary.* His latest book is *The Grand Jihad: How Islam and the Left Sabotage America* (2010).

Charles Murray is the W. H. Brady Scholar at the American Enterprise Institute and coauthor of the *New York Times* best selling book *The Bell Curve* (1994). His other works include *In Our Hands* (2006), *Real Education* (2008), and, most recently, *Coming Apart* (2012).

James Panero is the Managing Editor of *The New Criterion* where he writes on art and culture monthly and serves as the magazine's gallery critic. He is a contributor to numerous publications including *The Wall Street Journal, City Journal, New York* magazine, *Philanthropy, New York Daily News, The New York Post, Forbes, Arts & Antiques,* and *National Review.*

James Piereson is a senior fellow at the Manhattan Institute, president of the William E. Simon Foundation, and former executive director and trustee of the John M. Olin Foundation. He has written for multiple publications and his books include *Camelot and the Cultural Revolution: How the Assassination of John F. Kennedy Shattered American Liberalism* (2007) and *The Pursuit of Liberty: Can the Ideals That Made America Great Provide a Model for the World* (2008).

Andrew Roberts, a Fellow of the Royal Society of Literature, is a British historian and journalist. He is the author of *A History of the English-Speaking Peoples Since 1900* (2008) and *Masters and Commanders: How Roosevelt, Churchill, Marshall and Alanbrooke Won the War in the West* (2010). His latest book is the prize-winning *The Storm of War: A New History of the Second World War* (2012).

Kevin D. Williamson is a roving correspondent for *National Review* and a former program director at the Institute for Humane Studies. He writes regularly for *The New Criterion* and is the author of *The Politically*

Incorrect Guide to Socialism (2011), *The Dependency Agenda* (2012), and *The End of Politics* (2013).

Index

Index